p

_____

From:

_____

Date:

_____

Published by Barbour Books, an imprint of Barbour Publishing, Inc., 1810 Barbour Drive, Uhrichsville, Ohio 44683, www.barbourbooks.com

Our mission is to inspire the world with the life-changing message of the Bible.

Member of the
Evangelical Christian
Publishers Association

Printed in the United States of America.

POWER PRAYERS
for
Moms

Rachel Quillin

BARBOUR BOOKS
An Imprint of Barbour Publishing, Inc.

Contents

Introduction

The Power of Prayer

Motherhood! What an array of thoughts and emotions are evoked in that one word. One moment we tremble with joy; the next we are filled with trepidation. Motherhood is exhilarating and exhausting. Most of all, it is a privilege, a calling, and a responsibility we must never take lightly.

God wants to be involved in our lives as mothers. He knows there will be times fears overwhelm us. He's also aware that if we aren't careful, our pride will be our downfall. Only by placing Him first in our lives can we avoid these traps.

God realizes at times we will be tempted to focus on our children to the exclusion of other commitments— including Him and our marriages. He knows our strengths and weaknesses, and He wants to be invited to help us. That is why He tells us to pray. He desires to give us the wisdom and courage to be the mothers He means us to be.

God offered King Solomon anything he wanted, and what did Solomon request? Wisdom! He recognized that although he was chosen to lead Israel, they were God's people, and he needed God's help to govern them.

Our children also belong to the Lord. We must daily commit our children to Him. We also must commit ourselves to training them properly, providing for their emotional, physical, and spiritual needs. Moreover, we must commit our marriages and ministries to the Lord's care.

The only way for us to be good mothers is to first

give ourselves completely over to God. Daily we must seek His presence; only then will He be able to truly use us. In her book *The Power of a Praying Parent*, Stormie Omartian says, "We were to depend on God to enable us to raise our child properly, and He would see to it that our child's life was blessed."[1]

Thousands of years ago, Hannah, the mother of the prophet Samuel, recognized this truth as she prayed, "O LORD of hosts, if thou wilt indeed look on the affliction of thine handmaid, and remember me, and not forget thine handmaid, but wilt give unto thine handmaid a man child, then I will give him unto the LORD all the days of his life" (1 Samuel 1:11).

Besides praying for our children, we also must teach them to pray. John Drescher says, "When we foster prayer in family settings, we develop active and engaged spirituality. Such dedication to God reaches into all of life now and in the future."[2]

As we prepare our children for the future, we'll do our best to equip them for the battles they will face. After the apostle Paul describes the spiritual armor God has provided for us, he concludes with this admonition: "Praying always with all prayer and supplication in the Spirit" (Ephesians 6:18).

The first step in teaching our children about prayer is to let them see how important it is to us. Their attitudes largely will be determined by our own. If they see that spending time with God is a priority for us, they too will make it a priority.

Prayer *is* powerful. Helen Smith Shoemaker, cofounder of the Anglican Fellowship of Prayer, calls prayer "spiritual dynamite." Do you want this power? Then pray! Teach your children to pray.

I will never forget the simple, sincere prayer of my daughter when she was three years old. I was going through a difficult time, and as I wiped tears from my eyes, she asked, "Mommy, what's wrong?"

I told her, "Mommy is hurting right now, honey. Just pray for me."

Without hesitation she bowed her head and said, "Dear Jesus, please help Mommy feel better."

The answer was immediate. God didn't make the problem go away, but He eased the pain.

Young children will thank God for whatever they consider a blessing. We have much to learn from their innocence.

My oldest son recently got his first full-sized tooth brush. He had decided he was too big for the kid version. That night his prayer was simple yet sincere: "Thank You, God, for my big-people toothbrush." Although we may chuckle, I think God rejoices in the heartfelt thanksgiving of a child. He knows as that child develops his prayer life, he will do great things for God.

Teach children to pray when they are young, and they will continue the habit throughout their lives. They will pray for you throughout life's storms. They will thank God for you and for their other blessings. Teaching your children to pray is not only a responsibility; it is one of the greatest gifts you can give them.

We also need to pray for ourselves. It is not selfish to seek God's guidance. It is appropriate to beseech Him for strength, grace, and forgiveness. And it is imperative that we thank God for His many blessings and involve Him in every area of our lives. To live a fulfilling life, we must pray—for our children, our husbands, others, and even ourselves.

How to Use This Book

Power Prayers for Mothers is a guide to help you develop a more intimate walk with your heavenly Father. It is divided into chapters according to topics relevant to mothers, such as parenting and other areas of daily life. Read them in order or start with the topic of your choice.

Each prayer includes a scripture reference. In *Becoming the Woman I Want to Be*, Donna Partow says, "When you not only base your prayer requests on Scripture but actually turn Scripture into prayer, you don't have to worry whether or not you are praying according to God's will—you are."[3]

So read and apply the scriptures. Allow the prayers to become your own. Keep a pen and notebook handy to record your own thoughts and prayers. When appropriate, you might share selections with your child as you teach her to pray. If your child is a teen or adult, make her your prayer partner. As you grow closer to the Lord, you will become closer to one another.

Most important, spend time in prayer daily. It is vital to your relationship with God and with those around you. I fervently hope you will more fully experience the power of prayer. May God bless you in this endeavor!

Let us therefore come boldly unto the throne of grace, that we may obtain mercy, and find grace to help in time of need.

HEBREWS 4:16

Notes

1. Stormie Omartian, *The Power of a Praying Parent* (Eugene, OR: Harvest House, 2007), 18.

2. John M. Drescher, *Parents Passing the Torch of Faith* (Scottdale, PA: Herald Press, 1997), 52.

3. Donna Partow, *Becoming the Woman I Want to Be* (Bloomington, MN: Bethany House, 2004), 2.

The Power of Unconditional Love

God established His plan of salvation even before the world began. He knew we would sin, and He created us anyway. Revelation 13:8 calls Jesus "the Lamb slain from the foundation of the world." Jesus knew He would be the sacrifice who would pay for our sins. He understood He would leave the glory of heaven and take up residence in this evil-infested world. He was prepared to be rejected by many whom He loved. By far, the worst thing He would endure would be His Father's rejection as He was covered with our sins. Yes, Christ knew before creation what part He would play. It was horrible but necessary, and He was willing.

Why then do so many reject Him or try to get to heaven on their own merit? Christ did all that needs to be done. Our part is simply to accept Him. Certainly He will begin to change us once we trust Him as our Savior, but that is a result of salvation, not the cause of it.

Matthew 18:3 says, "Verily I say unto you, Except ye be converted, and become as little children, ye shall not enter into the kingdom of heaven." What a blessing it is to see a child bow before the God of the universe and to trust Him as Savior! But it is equally thrilling when an adult becomes as trusting as a child and seeks God's forgiveness. Ardell was eighty-two when she found Jesus. Although she had taught Sunday school, she didn't truly know the salvation of the Lord. What a difference it made when she accepted Him.

What is your position with Jesus? Do you know Him as Savior, or are you trying to be righteous on your own? Do you understand how offensive your sin is to our holy God? Romans 3:10 says, "There is none righteous, no, not one." All of us are sinners, and because of this we deserve death—eternal punishment in hell. "For the wages of sin is death; but the gift of God is eternal life through Jesus Christ our Lord" (Romans 6:23).

Did you notice the word "but"? Yes, we deserve death, *but* God loved us so much that even before He made us, He established a plan to save us. Still, salvation is not automatic. Our part is to call on Christ (Romans 10:10).

If you have committed your life to Christ, rejoice! You have the greatest of blessings. If you've never trusted Christ, won't you do it today? If you reject Him, nothing else in this book matters. Having a clean heart before God and helping your children to have the same are the greatest gifts you can give them. Carefully consider that as you read the following passages.

Seek Christ Now

Seek ye the Lord while he may be found,
call ye upon him while he is near.

ISAIAH 55:6

How You long to save the lost and dying, Lord Jesus!
How eager You are to cleanse us from our sins. From the
sweet voices of tiny children to the final breaths of elderly
grandparents, the plea for forgiveness and salvation fills You
with delight. Oh Father, may many more people seek You
while You may be found.

Don't Let the Little Ones Perish

Even so it is not the will of your Father which is in heaven,
that one of these little ones should perish.

MATTHEW 18:14

Lord, I'm so glad You often used children in Your teachings
and emphasized the importance of bringing them to You.
Otherwise we might fail to share Your salvation with them. I
remember how excited I was as a small child when I gave my
life to You. When my children recognized Your salvation was
for them, my heart sang. What a precious gift—Your love for
children.

A Prayer of Christ

Father, the hour is come; glorify thy Son, that thy Son also may
glorify thee: as thou hast given him power over all flesh, that he
should give eternal life to as many as thou hast given him. And
this is life eternal, that they might know thee the only true God,
and Jesus Christ, whom thou hast sent. I have glorified thee on
the earth: I have finished the work which thou gavest me to do.

JOHN 17:1–4

Saved through Christ Alone

Neither is there salvation in any other: for there is none other name under heaven given among men, whereby we must be saved.

ACTS 4:12

Lord Jesus, how sad You must be when You see the pride that consumes humanity. The gift of salvation was a great sacrifice for You, but now it is readily available to us. Yet so many people try to save themselves. Some call on You for their salvation but trust in themselves to work out the details. Others live only for the moment and refuse to acknowledge their need. I'm so glad You saved me, Lord. Thank You for eternal life!

Belief, Confession, Salvation

If thou shalt confess with thy mouth the Lord Jesus, and shalt believe in thine heart that God hath raised him from the dead, thou shalt be saved. For with the heart man believeth unto righteousness; and with the mouth confession is made unto salvation.

ROMANS 10:9–10

Lord, when I look at what You're saying about how I can be saved, I'm amazed. Father, prepare more hearts to believe in Jesus. Let more people confess that You alone can save. How wonderful it would be if all of my children would accept You!

Seeing Salvation

And he came by the Spirit into the temple: and when the parents brought in the child Jesus, to do for him after the custom of the law, then took he him up in his arms, and blessed God, and said, Lord, now lettest thou thy servant depart in peace, according to thy word: for mine eyes have seen thy salvation.

LUKE 2:27–30

White as Snow

Come now, and let us reason together, saith the LORD:
though your sins be as scarlet, they shall be as white as snow;
though they be red like crimson, they shall be as wool.

ISAIAH 1:18

My children love snow so much they've requested it as early
as September. Father, You know how my husband and I
chuckled about that. You know how we considered praying
that it would hold off until Christmas. Yet when it came to
our children having their hearts washed "white as snow," we
were eager to see it happen. It became a time of rejoicing for
all of us.

Saved for Christ's Purpose

[God] hath saved us, and called us with an holy calling,
not according to our works, but according to his own purpose and
grace, which was given us in Christ Jesus before the world began.

2 TIMOTHY 1:9

Oh great God, before You spoke this world into existence, You
had me in mind. You knew I would fail and need cleansing,
and You had a plan. You gave Your Son to pay the price for
my sin. I cannot fathom the depth of Your love. I've borne
more than one child, and I can't imagine sacrificing any of
them, but You did. How passionate Your love is!

In a Looking Glass

*But we all, with open face beholding as in a glass the glory
of the Lord, are changed into the same image from glory
to glory, even as by the Spirit of the Lord.*

2 Corinthians 3:18

You are changing me, Lord, and I'm glad. The more I see
You, the more I become like You. It's a work You began
when You agreed to go to the cross for my sins. To be identified with You is the utmost privilege. Oh, what a glorious
day is coming when I become like You; for I will see You as
You are!

Work It Out

*Wherefore, my beloved, as ye have always obeyed, not as
in my presence only, but now much more in my absence,
work out your own salvation with fear and trembling.*

Philippians 2:12

Almighty God, Your salvation ensures I will spend eternity
with You rather than in hell, but it means so much more than
that. I am saved to bring glory to Your name and enjoy Your
presence. You have a plan for me now that You've given this
marvelous gift. I must honor and live for You. I must bring
others to You.

False Zeal

For I bear them record that they have a zeal of God,
but not according to knowledge.

ROMANS 10:2

Dear God, there are many religious people who know there has to be a higher being, but that's the only understanding they have. They are afraid they will offend this "god," so they make up a religion to avoid it. Some people are relying on religious beliefs that have no scriptural backing. Help me to share Your truth so more people will be saved.

Taking Up My Cross

And he said to them all, If any man will come after me,
let him deny himself, and take up his cross daily, and follow me.

LUKE 9:23

You have given me eternal life, Jesus, and no one can take it from me. There's nothing I can do that will make me more or less saved. Still, I will live for You.

So many people don't understand this commitment. I want to be identified with You though, precious Savior, and if that requires being misunderstood, mocked, or even persecuted, I am willing.

You Brought Me Out of Bondage

And thou shalt shew thy son in that day, saying, This is done because of that which the Lord did unto me when I came forth out of Egypt.
EXODUS 13:8

Great Deliverer, I was enslaved in the worst way. Sin held me captive, and I could not break free, but in Your grace and mercy You freed me. I want to be a living testament to the victory You won in my soul.

My children need to see this. They need to understand the bondage of sin and the freedom they can have in You. My testimony will draw my children and grandchildren to You.

Christ Can Save

Wherefore he is able also to save them to the uttermost that come unto God by him, seeing he ever liveth to make intercession for them.
HEBREWS 7:25

I've known a lot of bad people, Jesus. Although I must not embrace their lifestyles, I can show them Your love. It isn't my place to decide who is worthy of Your grace. I must share You with everyone I meet. Help me to be an example to my children of the truth that Your salvation is for all who come to You.

The Power of the Living Word

*And he came to Nazareth, where he had been brought up:
and, as his custom was, he went into the synagogue
on the sabbath day, and stood up for to read.*
LUKE 4:16

Jesus, the living Word of God, loved sharing scripture with those He came to save. He understood the powerful influence the Bible would have on their lives if they willingly received it.

We sometimes forget what a great gift we have, and we take our Bibles for granted. It's easy for us to purchase Bibles or even get them for free, but it's not that way for all believers. Bibles are smuggled into some places or secretly printed. Some people groups do not have Bibles in their native tongue. And there are still some people who do not even have a written language.

What they wouldn't give to have just a portion of God's precious Word! Yet many of us take it for granted. We grab our Bible on Sunday morning and ignore it the rest of the week. Or we may give it a cursory glance on other days with little concern for what it says. We often leave our children's Bible training to their Sunday school teachers and pastors. Few of us actually pore over scripture seriously.

Oh, how God wants mothers who will study and live

by the Bible! He wants so much for us to find strength from His Word. What pleasure He gains when He sees a mom mentoring her child spiritually and sharing daily devotions with him.

We have great riches both in God's Word and in our children. Let's not take them lightly. The following passages deal with many aspects of God's Word. Read them carefully, and renew or establish your commitment to cherish the Bible.

Perfection

As for God, his way is perfect; the word of the LORD
is tried: he is a buckler to all them that trust in him.

2 SAMUEL 22:31

Your way is perfect, oh Lord. You will never steer me wrong.
When I face confusion in my life, I wonder what my next step
should be, but Your Word guides me. It answers my questions
about life, tells me how to handle relationships, instructs me
in my role as a mother, and encourages me daily. You have
truly given me all I need to succeed.

Sharing with My Children

And that from a child thou hast known the holy scriptures, which are able
to make thee wise unto salvation through faith which is in Christ Jesus.

2 TIMOTHY 3:15

What a tremendous privilege I have to be able to share Your
Word with my children, dear God. It is an abundance of
spiritual wealth right at our fingertips. Through scripture
we can know Your great salvation and experience a deeper
understanding of Your immense love for us. It is a prize to
be treasured. Let us care for our Bibles, though the pages are
worn from constant use!

Words from God

I have manifested thy name unto the men which thou gavest me out of the
world: thine they were, and thou gavest them me; and they have kept thy
word. Now they have known that all things whatsoever thou hast given
me are of thee. For I have given unto them the words which thou gavest
me; and they have received them, and have known surely that I came
out from thee, and they have believed that thou didst send me.

JOHN 17:6–8

The Comfort of the Scriptures

*For whatsoever things were written aforetime were
written for our learning, that we through patience
and comfort of the scriptures might have hope.*

Romans 15:4

Lord, the world is not as You intended. You wanted us to glorify You—to have fellowship with You. Our twisted, sinful natures have caused sorrow and hate, fear and confusion. In Your great love You've given me a way to have hope and comfort. You gave Your Word so I might learn how to have a restored relationship with You. I don't have to be defeated by the attitudes of this world. Through Your Word You've given me a better way.

Life through Christ's Name

*But these are written, that ye might believe that Jesus is the Christ,
the Son of God; and that believing ye might have life through his name.*

John 20:31

We're such visual people, God. We should be able to accept who You are simply by faith, but You know how our minds work. We hold firm to the old saying "Seeing is believing." Even during biblical times people wanted a sign from You to prove who You were. So You gave us Your Word—a record of Your mighty acts—to help us know and believe in You. You looked ahead and saw what we would need, and You provided it.

No Void Returns

*So shall my word be that goeth forth out of my mouth: it shall not
return unto me void, but it shall accomplish that which I please,
and it shall prosper in the thing whereto I sent it.*

Isaiah 55:11

Your Word is so effective, Father. Nothing is more powerful. Oh God, if by Your Word You spoke the world into existence, how can I doubt the power it can have in my life? How can I question whether it will influence the lives of my children?

Let us feast on God's Word daily. It will do a great work in us, for He has promised His Word will not return unto Him void.

Safety in God's Word

*Every word of God is pure: he is a shield
unto them that put their trust in him.*

PROVERBS 30:5

Many dangers are lurking nearby, dear God. People hate me for the stand I take for You. Satan hurls trials and temptations at me, but in Your Word I find strength and safety. I know my children are facing this adversary as well. Remind them they have protection in You. They've relied on plastic swords and shields for their mock battles, but safety from the real foe lies in Your Word.

Hearing versus Doing

*But be ye doers of the word, and not
hearers only, deceiving your own selves.*

JAMES 1:22

Father, sometimes my children only seem like they understand what I am saying. They might even acknowledge or repeat my words, but they fail to put them into practice. Their behavior frustrates me at times, but I have to wonder how You must feel. You've given me the Bible to guide and protect me, yet I fail to live by it. Forgive me, Lord. Make me a doer of Your Word—not just a hearer.

God's Word Won't Change

Ye shall not add unto the word which I command you,
neither shall ye diminish ought from it, that ye may keep the
commandments of the LORD your God which I command you.

DEUTERONOMY 4:2

Your Word is established forever, almighty God. A mere mortal, I've no business adding to or taking away from it. I would never deliberately take a pen and scratch through the parts that convict me. I wouldn't add words or lines here and there, but sometimes my life becomes that writing instrument as I choose to do my own thing. Forgive me, Father. I want my life to represent You according to Your whole Word—not just the parts I'm comfortable with.

Meditation

This book of the law shall not depart out of thy mouth;
but thou shalt meditate therein day and night, that thou mayest
observe to do according to all that is written therein: for then thou
shalt make thy way prosperous, and then thou shalt have good success.

JOSHUA 1:8

So many things demand my focus and attention, dear Jesus. There are times I'm not even sure how to handle situations. I love my children, and I know motherhood is a tremendous blessing. I want to do a good job with my family, and I'm grateful You've given me the Bible as my guidebook. As I pore over each passage, it becomes more and more obvious that You want to help me succeed.

Keeping God's Word

Blessed is he that readeth, and they that hear
the words of this prophecy, and keep those things
which are written therein: for the time is at hand.

REVELATION 1:3

I know that my time on earth is limited and that what I do for You counts more than anything else. I've tried to instill this conviction in my children, but ultimately it is You who will show them the importance of reading and living Your Word. All I can do is set the right example. I want Your blessing in my life and in the lives of my children. Help me to passionately study and obey Your commands.

Hearing Leads to Trusting

So then faith cometh by hearing,
and hearing by the word of God.
ROMANS 10:17

I want my children to trust in You, Father, and I know You've given me the opportunity to be directly involved in their faith. I'm going to share Your Word with them daily. I will encourage them to memorize passages consistently. I commit to pray for their salvation and surrender them to You. Being able to take part in spreading the truths of the Gospel is an amazing privilege. Lord, You've done so much for me; I want to give back to You.

Long-Lasting Word

Be ye mindful always of his covenant; the word
which he commanded to a thousand generations.
1 CHRONICLES 16:15

I've had an old hymn running through my mind. It speaks of good, old-fashioned religion. One stanza says, "It was good for my mother and father, and it's good enough for me." I guess I don't know about "religion," so to speak, but Your Word was good for my parents and grandparents and generations before them. It's wonderful for me and my children and the generations to follow. Your Word is all I need.

Growing Daily

As newborn babes, desire the sincere milk
of the word, that ye may grow thereby.

I stared at my newborn son, dear God, and watched him eagerly nursing. Oh, how often he wanted that nourishing milk—every two hours it seemed. I delighted in that tiny bundle of love, and it brought great joy to see him grow—to know I'd had a part in that miracle. Father, let me desire Your Word just as my son delighted in that milk. Let it nourish and sustain me and bring continued growth.

The Power of a Job Well Done

Have you ever wished for more hours in a day? Come on, admit it! As mothers, we could all use a little extra time. We could probably break our responsibilities into five main categories: God, home/family, church, job, and miscellaneous. Looking at them that way, they don't seem terribly overwhelming. But, oh, the subcategories and minor subdivisions.

Let's see. I need to spend time with God today—He really deserves more than my leftover attention. But there's much to do! Today's my husband's birthday, so I need to make a cake and nice dinner and get his gift ready. Maybe the kids could make a cute banner and help me hang the balloons. Oh, and my three-year-old has almost reached his summer reading goal. He only needs forty-five minutes, but the summer reading program ends tomorrow! All the kids need baths, and I really need to at least surface-clean the house. After all, my neatnik brother is coming after work.

At church tonight we have vacation Bible school. True, I'm only helping out, but it is the three- and four-year-old class, full of adorable but ornery little boys. It leaves me exhausted, so I'd better not plan on doing much when I get home late tonight. I really need to compile the list of needed supplies for the upcoming junior-church quarter. My devotional project needs to be completed, and I need to prepare samples for other work. I'll have to do that while the children are sleeping (and I hear them stirring now!). Oh, and I need to mow the grass, weed the garden, pick and freeze the beans, get the kids' school lessons together, get ready for next week's mini-vacation (do I really have time for vacation?). . .

Do your thoughts sound anything like this? Even though our lists might vary, the basic structure is similar. Our schedules don't even leave room for changes in plans that inevitably occur. You know what I mean: sick children, broken dishwashers, unexpected guests. It's all part of being a mom. We have a choice in how we handle these situations though. We can let ourselves become stressed as we attempt to do things alone, or we can hand the list over to God and ask Him for strength, wisdom, and clarity of mind to do the work He has given us in the best way possible. He'll gladly help us through it all and allow us to experience the power of a job well done.

Little or Much?

For unto every one that hath shall be given,
and he shall have abundance: but from him that
hath not shall be taken away even that which he hath.

MATTHEW 25:29

Motherhood is a big responsibility, Father. I have to make sure my family is eating right and properly clothed. I need to keep track of all of their schedules and appointments. I must ensure that they are active in church and are being spiritually fed. I'm thankful for these tasks, Lord. You wouldn't give them to me if I weren't capable of managing them. Let me prove worthy of Your trust.

Have Courage

Only be thou strong and very courageous, that thou mayest
observe to do according to all the law, which Moses my
servant commanded thee: turn not from it to the right hand
or to the left, that thou mayest prosper withersoever thou goest.

JOSHUA 1:7

When I learned I was expecting a child, so many emotions engulfed me. I was both awed and terrified. I wanted the baby desperately, but I was fearful I wouldn't know how to care for him properly. But You encouraged me, Lord. "Be strong; have courage," You said. "I am with you," was Your reminder. You always have been there for me—and for my child—and You always will.

Christ's Responsibilities

I have glorified thee on the earth: I have finished the work which thou gavest me to do. And now, O Father, glorify thou me with thine own self with the glory which I had with thee before the world was. I have manifested thy name unto the men which thou gavest me out of the world: thine they were, and thou gavest them me; and they have kept thy word.

JOHN 17:4–6

Being a Witness

But ye shall receive power, after that the Holy Ghost is come upon you: and ye shall be witnesses unto me both in Jerusalem, and in all Judaea, and in Samaria, and unto the uttermost part of the earth.

ACTS 1:8

Sometimes I try to make excuses for why I can't witness to one person or another, but in my heart I know this is wrong, and it sets a bad example for my children. I need to obey Your command to share Your love with others and to trust Your promise that the Holy Spirit will be with me. I might be the only one who will present the Gospel to those You place in my path.

Send Me

Also I heard the voice of the Lord, saying, Whom shall I send, and who will go for us? Then said I, Here am I; send me.

ISAIAH 6:8

Master, send me. Send me to my neighbor who is grieving over a situation beyond her control; let me comfort her. Send me to my children; I want to apply kisses and Band-Aids to their hurts. Send me to someone who needs to hear about Your offer of salvation so I can share Your love with her. Here am I, Lord. Send me wherever there is a need I can help meet.

I Will Live a Godly Life

Denying ungodliness and worldly lusts, we should live soberly,
righteously, and godly, in this present world.
TITUS 2:12

Dear God, I'm not sure how many times I've heard that if my love for You is what it should be, all other areas of my life will line up properly. I don't really get tired of hearing it though. The world offers foolish but often attractive temptations, and I must consciously turn away from them; for everything I do affects someone else—my husband or children, my friends or neighbors. I will choose daily to live in a godly manner.

I Want to Be Salty

Ye are the salt of the earth: but if the salt have lost his savour,
wherewith shall it be salted? it is thenceforth good for nothing,
but to be cast out, and to be trodden under foot of men.
MATTHEW 5:13

I've been disappointed after departing from a drive-through and discovering there was no salt in the bag. Half my fries went uneaten because they didn't taste as good without salt. It's only fitting that You would use my favorite seasoning to remind me of my responsibility to You and to those who are lost without You. I want the world to see how good Your love tastes. Please help me to be salty!

God's Kingdom First

But seek ye first the kingdom of God, and his righteousness;
and all these things shall be added unto you.

MATTHEW 6:33

It's really a matter of priorities, isn't it, Jesus? I have so many responsibilities—to You, to my husband and kids, to my church and community; and sometimes I get things out of order. All of these people are so important to me, and I want to be a blessing to all of them. I just need to remember that Your kingdom must come first. If I would get that right, I wouldn't have as much trouble taking care of the rest.

Excuses Anger God

And Moses said unto God, Who am I, that I should go unto Pharaoh, and
that I should bring forth the children of Israel out of Egypt? . . . O my
LORD, I am not eloquent, neither heretofore, nor since thou hast spoken
unto thy servant: but I am slow of speech, and of a slow tongue. And the
LORD said unto him, Who hath made man's mouth? or who maketh the
dumb, or deaf, or the seeing, or the blind? have not I the LORD?

EXODUS 3:11; 4:10–11

Keeping God's Commands

And hereby we do know that we know him,
if we keep his commandments.

1 JOHN 2:3

Father, my life should tell people You are important to me. I say I love You, but I need to joyfully obey You too. I'm pleased when my son wraps his arms around my neck and proclaims his love for me, but when he does so after willingly obeying me, it just sweetens the deal. Father, I want others to see and hear that You mean much to me.

Eating the Fruit

Say ye to the righteous, that it shall be well with him:
for they shall eat the fruit of their doings.

ISAIAH 3:10

I enjoy a good meal, Father, and I know my family appreciates when I take the time to prepare a nice dinner, but sometimes I fail to notice the clock and we end up eating peanut butter. That's true in other areas too. If I fulfill the responsibilities You give me, I am blessed—and others are too. If I neglect this work, we all suffer. Help me to be responsible.

Judged Accordingly

Now he that planteth and he that watereth are one: and every
man shall receive his own reward according to his own labour.

I CORINTHIANS 3:8

God, I was reminded of this important truth today. When I do well, You accept my work, but when I shirk my duties, I pay the consequences. My son was angry that his sister received dessert and he didn't. I reminded him that if he had helped clear the table, then he too would have enjoyed ice cream. I hope he learned a lesson, and I pray I'll remember it too!

Before I Was Formed

*Before I formed thee in the belly I knew thee; and before
thou camest forth out of the womb I sanctified thee.*

JEREMIAH 1:5

It never ceases to amaze me, Lord, that even before I was
conceived, You knew the work You had for me to do. I'm just
now learning what these responsibilities are. I've discovered
one of my roles is to be a good mother. You already know
the plan You have for my children as well, and part of Your
design for me is to help mold them into people who will carry
out Your design for them.

Be Prepared

*And when he was at the place, he said unto them,
Pray that ye enter not into temptation.*

LUKE 22:40

It's inevitable, isn't it, Jesus? Even You had to face temptations.
At least once, You spent forty days praying and facing these
situations. If You needed to seek Your Father, how much more
do I need to pray? Lord, I ask You to help me stand strong
when temptations come, and please be with my children
when they too must choose right from wrong.

The Power of a Helpmeet

This is now bone of my bones, and flesh of my flesh. . . .
Therefore shall a man leave his father and his mother,
and shall cleave unto his wife: and they shall be one flesh.
GENESIS 2:23–24

Marriage is a sacred union God established in the earliest days of creation. If He felt it was important way back then, we must take it seriously now.

Marriage has several purposes. First, God saw that it wasn't good for man to be alone, so He created for him a helpmeet. Often we combine the words *help* and *meet*, but they really are separate. God made Eve for Adam so she could help meet his needs physically, spiritually, and emotionally. She wasn't created to be his slave. She was created to be his other half. He wasn't complete without her. When they were joined in marriage, they became one flesh—one complete unit working as a whole.

Think about it this way: In a healthy body, the legs can't do all the work while walking up a mountain path. The eyes are needed to see the trail ahead. The arms help balance; the back gives support. Ears are alert for danger, and every other body part functions as it was designed to. Although that hike will present challenges and perhaps difficulties, when everything works together as it should, the experience is deeply rewarding. The same is true in marriage and family relationships. Each member has certain gifts and abilities to contribute. When all members do their part, the results are beautiful.

"I don't have a healthy marriage or family," you might say. Give your situation to the Lord, and He will give You wisdom to know how to handle it. If you do your part, God is sure to bless you. It might not be exactly how you think He will, but watch to see what He has in store for you.

God also uses marriage as a picture of the union between Christ and the church (Ephesians 5:21–33). The husband is to represent Christ, while the wife is the picture of the church. When the church works together with Christ and all of us do our parts, great things are accomplished for Christ's kingdom.

Make sure you are doing your part both as a wife to your husband and as the bride of Christ. Doing so will help strengthen you as a mother. Pray daily—more than once a day—that God will help you be a godly wife.

The following prayers are meant to help you get started, but search the scriptures to discover what else God has for you as a wife. Then pray and live accordingly.

My Beloved

I am my beloved's, and my beloved is mine.
Song of Solomon 6:3

My heart is too full for words, Father. I can't fully express how blessed I am to have my husband. His love is constant; he is by my side in every situation. He laughs with me. He offers strength and encouragement. His children adore him; other people respect him. More and more, we two become one. He is truly a gift, and I thank You.

Submitting

Submitting yourselves one to another in the fear of God.
Ephesians 5:21

I haven't met many people who like the word *submit*, and I have a feeling You've noticed this too, Lord. I think we often misconstrue submission as slavery. Submission doesn't come easily. Most people are somewhat self-centered. It doesn't come naturally to put others ahead of ourselves, but when we consider what is best for our family, submission becomes a pleasure rather than bondage.

Lift Up One Another

Knowledge puffeth up, but charity edifieth.
1 Corinthians 8:1

It has been said that too often the ones we love the most are the ones we hurt the most deeply. Why is that, Father? Are we too familiar with the people in these intimate relationships that we aren't careful, or do we just expect them to love us enough to understand? Father, please forgive me for the times I've hurt my husband and children. I should lift them up. I should make them feel cherished. By Your grace, I will.

Am I a Good Gift?

House and riches are the inheritance of fathers:
and a prudent wife is from the LORD.
PROVERBS 19:14

I know I often tend to point to verses that pertain to a husband's responsibilities to his wife and family, but my focus really should be on Your expectations of me. I know Your plan was for me and my husband to be joined. I was given to my husband by You. I want to be a source of joy to him. I want to make him glad that You chose me to be his life partner.

Negative Encouragement

And the man said, The woman whom thou
gavest to be with me, she gave me of the tree, and I did eat.
GENESIS 3:12

Lord, I know my husband is to be the spiritual leader in our home. You've given him that responsibility, but as a unit, we have influence with each other. Eve used her influence with Adam the wrong way, and the results were disastrous. Sarai did the same with Abram with horrible results. Let me learn from their mistakes. I resolve to encourage my husband to do right.

My Responsibilities

That they may teach the young women to be sober, to love
their husbands, to love their children, to be discreet, chaste,
keepers at home, good, obedient to their own husbands,
that the word of God be not blasphemed.
TITUS 2:4–5

We women tend to want to ignore passages telling us how we should serve our husbands. We interpret them as our sentence to slavery rather than as a means to bring unity to our families and glory to You. God, I have a role to fill. My husband does as well. Give us both wisdom to do what You've designed us to do so that we will strengthen our homes and honor You.

A Fruitful Marriage

But the fruit of the Spirit is love, joy, peace, longsuffering, gentleness, goodness, faith, meekness, temperance: against such there is no law.
GALATIANS 5:22–23

When my children want a snack, I like to give them fresh fruit. The natural sweetness satisfies, and the nutrients add goodness. I need those qualities in my marriage too, Father, and You've provided them in a marvelous way—through Your Holy Spirit. As my husband and I spend time with You, Your fruit ripens, and the quality of our marriage improves.

A Beautiful Adornment

A virtuous woman is a crown to her husband: but she that maketh ashamed is as rottenness in his bones.
PROVERBS 12:4

I have a choice. Either I can be a beautiful crown—someone my husband would be proud and honored to call his wife; or I can be rotten—a stinking cancer that will destroy our marriage. Dear Jesus, I know it depends on my attitude and my relationship with You. Only You can polish me into the shining ornament who will bless my husband, encourage others, and bring glory to You.

A Joyful Life

Live joyfully with the
wife whom thou lovest.
ECCLESIASTES 9:9

Do I make it easy for my husband to obey Your command to live joyfully with me, Father? There are so many things I could do that would fill our home with joy. I know even simple things like doing my best to look nice and keeping the home neat go a long way in providing a pleasant atmosphere. Showing love and respect for each person also is conducive to a good home life. Father, let us be joyful.

Speaking the Truth in Love

But speaking the truth in love, may [we] grow up
into him in all things, which is the head, even Christ.
EPHESIANS 4:15

Who likes to be reminded of her shortcomings? I know I don't, but sometimes I need the reminder. When my husband lovingly points out an area that needs work, I am more than willing to do something about it. It's another way in which we should follow Your example. You don't let us get away with wrong; instead, gently through scripture and the Holy Spirit, You guide us back to the right path.

Wedding Vows

What therefore God hath joined together,
let not man put asunder.
MARK 10:9

Father, so many of my friends have gone through the bitterness of divorce. For some, it was beyond their control. For others, it was their choice. In any case, I'm inclined to say, "But for the grace of God, there go I." I'm so thankful for a husband who loves You. I will not take lightly the blessing of a man who takes his wedding vows seriously. I recommit to loving my husband and being the wife I should be.

Not Good

*And the LORD God said, It is not good that the man
should be alone; I will make him an help meet for him.*
GENESIS 2:18

Dear God, You said, "It is not good that man should be alone." Man needed a helper—someone to complete him. So You performed an amazing operation and gave him a wife to be a blessing and to complement him. That is what I should be. My husband and I are one flesh. Help us to care for each other as such.

Lasting Love

*Many waters cannot quench love, neither can the floods
drown it: if a man would give all the substance of
his house for love, it would utterly be contemned.*
SONG OF SOLOMON 8:7

The love I have for my husband should be lasting, Lord. With Your help it will be. In Your eyes, there's no such thing as not being in love anymore. You made true love and marriage to last. Fill our lives with the abundance of this love. Let nothing destroy it!

The Marriage Feast

And he saith unto me, Write, Blessed are they which
are called unto the marriage supper of the Lamb.
And he saith unto me, These are the true sayings of God.
REVELATION 19:9

I remember how exciting it was to plan my wedding, Lord.
It took a good deal of effort, but it was a beautiful day. As I
reflect on that, I must consider how that day represents the
day You will claim Your bride. My marriage is to be a picture
of Your marriage too. You will be my Groom. Oh Jesus, let
me represent You well so others will also want to be Your
bride.

My Children

The Power of the Next Generation

In a book for mothers, a chapter such as this should be very near to our hearts. There are so many parts and stages of child-rearing that we could spend an hour or more in daily prayer just for our children.

Whether your children are infants or adults, they desperately need you to intercede to the heavenly Father on their behalf. As the time of Christ's return draws nearer, our children will face more trials and temptations. They will be bombarded with the humanistic teachings of this world, and they might be confused about what to believe.

Satan is hard at work. He employs outspoken people with a lot of charisma to convince people to believe anything other than what the Bible teaches. He is the master of deceit and often uses partial truths to get people to believe complete lies. He wants our children, and he attempts to gain control of them even from the earliest age.

We don't have to let Satan win though. With much prayer, diligent Bible training, and a godly example, we have a winning combination. You see, God wants our children too, and He is much more powerful than Satan. The sooner we introduce our children to God, the more time they will have to do great things for Him.

In a letter to his son, John Quincy Adams wrote, "So great is my veneration for the Bible, and so strong my belief, that when duly read and meditated on, it is of all books in the world, that which contributes most to make men good, wise, and happy—that the earlier my children begin to read it, the more steadily they pursue the practice of reading it throughout their lives, the more lively and confident will be my hopes that they will prove useful citizens of their country, respectable members of society, and a real blessing to their parents."

This world needs godly parents banding together to dedicate themselves to rearing God-honoring individuals. Working together, we can give godliness and purity a strong voice. God can use us and our commitment to raising children His way to start a raging fire of revival throughout this nation. Are you willing to be part of this? It won't be easy, but it will be exciting. Recommit today to praying for and with your kids and grandkids. Share God's Word with them, and be the best Christian example You can be. God is eagerly waiting to bless parents who are willing to serve Him.

Olive Plants

Thy wife shall be as a fruitful vine by the sides of thine house:
thy children like olive plants round about thy table.

PSALM 128:3

You know how much my children love olives, Lord. We often joke that the kids are going to turn into olive plants. But when You compare my children to olive plants, You are making a more important point. You are reminding me of the importance of my children to my daily life. And just as olive oil was an offering to You, I must offer my children back to You to be used for Your glory.

Obedience and Blessing

And it shall come to pass, if thou shalt hearken diligently unto the
voice of the LORD thy God, to observe and to do all his commandments
which I command thee this day, that the LORD thy God will set thee
on high above all nations of the earth. . . . Blessed shall be the fruit
of thy body, and the fruit of thy ground, and the fruit of thy cattle,
the increase of thy kine, and the flocks of thy sheep.

DEUTERONOMY 28:1, 4

Oh wise God, all that You've commanded is for a purpose. You know what is best for me and for everyone else. You've promised that if I obey You, my children will be blessed. I could not give them a greater gift! Today, because I love You and because I want Your best for my children, I rededicate myself to living according to Your Word.

The Father's Business

And he said unto them, How is it that ye sought me?
wist ye not that I must be about my Father's business?

LUKE 2:49

You are truly their Father, and my children are called upon to do Your will. You've given them to me to nurture and train for a short while, but ultimately You will call them into service for You. When that time comes, help me give them to You completely, regardless of what You are asking. Help me not to fear, knowing that You are in control.

A Bitter Cry

And she was in bitterness of soul, and prayed unto the LORD,
and wept sore. And she vowed a vow, and said, O LORD of hosts,
if thou wilt indeed look on the affliction of thine handmaid,
and remember me, and not forget thine handmaid, but wilt give
unto thine handmaid a man child, then I will give him unto the LORD
all the days of his life, and there shall no razor come upon his head.

1 SAMUEL 1:10–11

Forbid Them Not

But Jesus said, Suffer little children, and forbid them not,
to come unto me: for of such is the kingdom of heaven.

MATTHEW 19:14

I need to take a lesson from You, Lord. How many times do I reject my children and their cries for attention because I'm too busy doing my own thing? I know I don't like to be ignored, and neither do they. My little ones need my love. They need to know they are important. Please help me to set aside my own needs, open my arms, and let my children come to me.

Right in God's Sight

Josiah was eight years old when he began to reign, and he reigned in Jerusalem one and thirty years. And he did that which was right in the sight of the LORD, and walked in the ways of David his father, and declined neither to the right hand, nor to the left.

2 CHRONICLES 34:1–2

Oh great Leader, there are many adults in power today who do evil in Your sight. That's how it was with Amon, the king of Judah, but when Josiah, Amon's eight-year-old son, came into power, he did what was right. I don't know who his godly example was, but someone had a good influence on him. Let me be that person to my children, so that it can be said of them that they do what is right in Your sight.

Another Woman's Son

And the child grew, and she brought him unto Pharaoh's daughter, and he became her son.

EXODUS 2:10

Loving Father, there are some precious children in my life whom I didn't give birth to. You've placed us all in a position where I will have an impact on their lives. You know situations like this can sometimes be a little difficult, but if handled properly they can also be rewarding. I lift this family up to You. May all we do please You.

Good Training

Train up a child in the way he should go:
and when he is old, he will not depart from it.

PROVERBS 22:6

This might be one of the hardest commands to obey, Lord. It's not that I don't want to train my children properly. It's just that sometimes I'm not sure I know how. I know they need boundaries and discipline to help them feel safe and make good decisions. Yet I don't want to suffocate them so that they reject both You and me. Please help me train them right.

A Heart-Wrenching Command

And he said, Take now thy son, thine only son Isaac, whom thou lovest,
and get thee into the land of Moriah; and offer him there for a burnt
offering upon one of the mountains which I will tell thee of.

GENESIS 22:2

Oh God, I don't know if Sarah realized what Abraham was doing that fateful day when he and Isaac left for Moriah, but surely she suspected—surely she saw in Abraham's eye that something was amiss. Perhaps her heart screamed, "Why is this happening?" We all go through it at some point. We even cry for You to stop the hurt, and You quietly remind us that You make all things beautiful in Your time.

Even a Child Can Overcome Evil

Ye are of God, little children, and have overcome them:
because greater is he that is in you, than he that is in the world.

1 JOHN 4:4

Father, the greatest thing I can do for my children is to introduce them to You. When You are involved in their lives, they can overcome evil. In this world they will face much negative peer pressure. They might even question what they really believe. Help us all to form a solid foundation of faith, so that when the devil attacks, they will say, "Get behind me, Satan; my God is greater than you."

A Grandmother's Influence

When I call to remembrance the unfeigned faith that
is in thee, which dwelt first in thy grandmother Lois,
and thy mother Eunice; and I am persuaded that in thee also.

2 TIMOTHY 1:5

Just how many people are in heaven with You today because of Lois's faith, dear God? How many people did young Timothy reach for You because he had godly examples in his grandmother and mother? I know it's important to directly share my faith with those around me, but don't let me underestimate the power of a positive influence on my children and grandchildren; for they will reach those I won't ever meet.

Give My Child Wisdom

Thine, O LORD is the greatness, and the power, and the glory, and the
victory, and the majesty: for all that is in the heaven and in the earth
is thine; thine is the kingdom, O LORD, and thou art exalted as head
above all. . . . And give unto Solomon my son a perfect heart, to keep
thy commandments, thy testimonies, and thy statutes, and to do all these
things, and to build the palace, for the which I have made provision.

1 CHRONICLES 29:11, 19

Playing Favorites

And Isaac loved Esau, because he did eat of
his venison: but Rebekah loved Jacob.
GENESIS 25:28

I watch with pride as my oldest child excels in sports. I can't help but marvel at the art his sister creates. My third child is a delight in all of his ornery ways, and the wet baby kisses of my youngest bring both tears and smiles. Each of my children has something special to offer, and though it's sometimes difficult, I don't want to play favorites. With Your help, I will love each child completely and unconditionally.

I Will Praise the Lord

And she conceived again, and bare a son:
and she said, Now will I praise the LORD.
GENESIS 29:35

What a blessing it is to witness the amazing event of a child's birth, Lord. When that child is one's own, the miracle becomes even more precious. Of course, the blessing doesn't stop at birth. Throughout the child's life there are many reasons to praise You. The opportunity to be a mother is one of the most special gifts I have ever enjoyed. With my whole heart I will praise You.

The Power of a Warm Welcome

One of the best-known Bible passages on the home is found in Luke 10:38–42. It is the story of Mary and Martha. As the story goes, Martha invited Jesus to be a guest in her home. She took an important first step, but then her priorities became a little mixed up. Luke tells us that when Jesus arrived, Martha got right down to business serving Him. Meanwhile, her sister Mary sat quietly listening to Jesus teach. This angered Martha.

"Lord, doesn't it bother You that my sister is just sitting there while I do all the work? Why don't You tell her to get busy and help me?" she complained.

Of course, Jesus didn't view things quite the way Martha did. "Mary knows what she needs to do. I won't take that from her," He said quietly.

The story ends there, but we can learn important lessons from it. Foremost is that Christ needs to be welcome in our homes. He should have membership status rather than just a guest's invitation. He should be part of all we do and all the decisions we make.

We also need to consider how we react to Christ's presence in our homes. As mothers we must have servants' hearts, meeting the needs of our husbands and children. Did you notice Christ never rebuked Martha for cooking and cleaning? Those jobs must be done, but not at the expense of our relationship with Jesus. Part of God's purpose in creating us was so He might have fellowship with us. That's hard to do if we are constantly washing dishes and scrubbing floors. Jesus doesn't mind if the floor goes unswept if it means we will be spending time with Him.

It's also important that we spend time with our husbands and children. I've talked to many people who have few memories of fun times with their moms. She was always too busy polishing the furniture or pulling weeds from immaculate flower beds (the children weren't allowed to help because they wouldn't have done it to her satisfaction).

Another trap we mothers sometimes fall into is serving others at the expense of our families. We do things for the church or school. We make meals for neighbors who are ill. We're so busy doing, doing, doing that we forget to *be* good moms.

Don't get me wrong—God expects us to be good stewards of our homes. He intends for us to have servants' hearts, but He also expects us to be good mothers. It's not as impossible as it might sound. Pray that God will give you strength to accomplish everything and wisdom to know how to put priorities in the right order. Above all, be sure Christ is honored by the way your home is run.

Happy Meals

Better is a dinner of herbs where love is,
than a stalled ox and hatred therewith.
PROVERBS 15:17

Lord, You provide what we need to eat, and I am thankful. Our meals might not be fancy, and we often dine on leftovers, but we regularly get servings of laughter as our children share their latest antics. What a special family affair each mealtime is! I'll gladly eat spaghetti rather than lobster if it means we are enjoying each other instead of worrying over how to pay the food bill.

Looking beyond the Present

So David received of her hand that which she had brought him,
and said unto her, Go up in peace to thine house; see, I
have hearkened to thy voice, and have accepted thy person.
1 SAMUEL 25:35

Abigail had a big problem, Lord, and You had a big plan for her. It must not have been easy for her to go against her churlish husband, but she did it anyway. Not only was she hospitable; she was wise. In taking a big risk, she prevented a bigger tragedy, and she was blessed for it. Father, give me the ability to manage my home with kindness and wisdom as well.

Well Reported

Well reported of for good works; if she have brought up children, if she
have lodged strangers, if she have washed the saints' feet, if she have
relieved the afflicted, if she have diligently followed every good work.
1 TIMOTHY 5:10

I want to have the reputation of devoting myself to every
good work, Father, and You've given me clear instructions for
how to develop this reputation. I need to raise my children
according to Your Word. I need to open my home to those in
need and care for other believers. I have ample opportunities
to do these things. Make me aware when these situations
arise, and show me how to follow through.

Open to Ministry

If ye have judged me to be faithful to the Lord,
come into my house, and abide there. And she constrained us.
ACTS 16:15

Dear God, the childhood memories I have of sharing our
home with missionaries and evangelists are clear and happy. I
learned so much from these men and women of God. It is my
desire to open my home once again to those who are serving
You. I want my own children to experience that blessing and
to welcome those in the ministry.

A Change in the Guest List

For I say unto you, that none of those men
which were bidden shall taste of my supper.

LUKE 14:24

Dear God, do You remember the time we invited in vain a bunch of kids into our home? They all had other things to do, and we were hurt by the myriad excuses. Other people did come though, and we had a good time with them instead. I guess I know a little of how You must feel when so many reject You, but You are glad when someone does accept Your invitation.

At Home with God and Family

And Ruth said, Intreat me not to leave thee, or to return from
following after thee: for whither thou goest, I will go; and where thou
lodgest, I will lodge: thy people shall be my people, and thy God my God.

RUTH 1:16

I'm so thankful You've given instruction and examples for how we are to live, Lord. Ruth has inspired me for as long as I have known her story. She left her home and chose to help Naomi, but more important, she chose You. How very important that choice is! You must be the center of our home. Please be part of everything we do.

Caring for the Lord

Then shall the righteous answer him, saying, Lord, when saw we
thee an hungred, and fed thee? or thirsty, and gave thee drink? When saw
we thee a stranger, and took thee in? or naked, and clothed thee? Or when
saw we thee sick, or in prison, and came unto thee? And the King shall
answer and say unto them, Verily I say unto you, Inasmuch as ye have done
it unto one of the least of these my brethren, ye have done it unto me.

MATTHEW 25:37–40

The Ways of the Home

She looketh well to the ways of her household,
and eateth not the bread of idleness.

PROVERBS 31:27

Dear God, so many people make jokes about the role of a wife and mother, but if it weren't important, You wouldn't have mentioned it. I need to take seriously my responsibilities to prepare meals, maintain my kids' schedules, clean the house, and so on. I can do this with a complaining heart, or I can consider each endeavor, no matter how small or great, an opportunity to express my love. Let me serve with a joyful heart!

Given to Hospitality

Distributing to the necessity of saints; given to hospitality.

ROMANS 12:13

Showing hospitality is part of Your perfect will, but it isn't always perfectly easy. It's not that I don't want people here. It's just that sometimes I fall behind in my domestic duties, and I'd be embarrassed for anyone to come. Please give me the organizational skills I need to care for my family, clean up after them, and still have a home I am willing to share with others.

Building Up My House

Every wise woman buildeth her house:
but the foolish plucketh it down with her hands.

PROVERBS 14:1

So many homes are being torn apart these days, both emotionally and physically. Selfish tempers flare. Hurtful words and drinking glasses are hurled. Faces and walls get punched. It's sad and a bit frightening. You are a wise God. I beg for wisdom to care for my home. Let me uplift my husband and children. I want love and peace to fill our home. Protect us from heated fights and broken glass.

A Prophet's Chamber

Let us make a little chamber, I pray thee, on the wall; and let us set for him there a bed, and a table, and a stool, and a candlestick: and it shall be, when he cometh to us, that he shall turn in thither.
2 KINGS 4:10

Our home belongs to You, Father. You've blessed us with a comfortable place to live, and we thank You. We know You might call us to use our home in an unusual way. Help us to know if and when You are leading us to do this, and give us willing hearts. Surely much joy will follow if we are good stewards of Your gifts. We want to share that joy with others.

Teachable Moments

And thou shalt teach them diligently unto thy children, and shalt talk of them when thou sittest in thine house, and when thou walkest by the way, and when thou liest down, and when thou risest up.
DEUTERONOMY 6:7

Great Master, I have many responsibilities to You and to my children. My primary task is to lovingly teach and live by the truths found in Your Word. Each command You've given is filled with love and purpose. My children need to know how to trust and please You. I understand that for this to take place, I must constantly be aware of the teachable moments You give me.

No Prejudice

But the stranger that dwelleth with you shall be unto you as
one born among you, and thou shalt love him as thyself; for ye
were strangers in the land of Egypt: I am the LORD your God.

LEVITICUS 19:34

It seems there is often no room in our hearts or homes for those who are "different." We've established such widely held stereotypes that barriers are hard to overcome. We forget that we don't belong here ourselves; our true home is heaven. You've told us to treat strangers as we would our own children. We'd never reject our own offspring or mock their differences. We must be kind to and care for the strangers among us.

Consistency in the Home

For I have told him that I will judge his house for ever for
the iniquity which he knoweth; because his sons made
themselves vile, and he restrained them not.

1 SAMUEL 3:13

God, please forgive me. I know there are times at home when I allow things I should not. I get busy, and I overlook things that should be corrected. I forget that those things learned (or not learned) at home will eventually appear elsewhere and could have a negative effect on many people. Please grant me the strength and patience to teach and discipline my children consistently so that they will always please You.

The Power of a Sound Body

Often as mothers we are tempted to set aside our own health needs and concerns because we are too busy focusing on what must be done for our families. Sure, for the first nine months of a child's existence we are more careful than at other times. We recognize that our habits, our sleep patterns, and our diet will directly affect that precious life growing within us.

Do you remember how specific the angel was when he spoke to Manoah and his wife concerning her months of pregnancy with Samson? "Thou shalt conceive, and bear a son. Now therefore beware, I pray thee, and drink not wine nor strong drink, and eat not any unclean thing" (Judges 13:3–4).

Once the baby is born, we tend to forget ourselves and focus on our child. To some extent that is necessary, but we must realize that our health continues to affect our child and others around us. When we allow ourselves to become exhausted, we become mentally unstable. Not only does that harm our attitude and cause us to say and do things we normally wouldn't say or do, it also affects areas such as our driving. We become dangerous to those in our vehicles as well as to others on the road.

In cases of severe sleep deprivation, depression might ensue. In the initial months after my first son was born, I was a nervous mom. My poor little boy sensed that, and he cried a good deal. I did too, and I slept very little.

2 Timothy 1:7 says, "For God hath not given us the spirit of fear; but of power, and of love, and of a sound mind." It's a beautiful promise, but often when we are overly tired, our minds are filled with fear and aren't very sound. I had to learn first that I needed to rely on God, and second that it's okay to ask for help. This is true when our children are young and when they get older. We don't automatically become superhuman when we become moms. Our own health needs attention, and the sooner we realize that, the more effective we'll be as mothers.

I've spoken mostly of getting quality rest because that's the area most often ignored. However, getting good nutrition and proper exercise is important too. This can be a big challenge because of time constraints, but there are several sneaky ways to incorporate them. It might require a little creativity, but in the long run it could save time as well as sanity.

A Sense of Humor

A merry heart doeth good like a medicine:
but a broken spirit drieth the bones.

PROVERBS 17:22

It sounds to me like You approve of—even encourage—a good laugh. I sometimes forget just how exhilarating it can be to laugh so hard it brings tears. My heart swells each time I hear my children playing together. I think of all the silly moments we have shared, and I am reminded of how those times refreshed the mind and soul. Oh God, fill our home with laughter.

Grace Sufficient

And lest I should be exalted above measure through the abundance of the revelations, there was given to me a thorn in the flesh, the messenger of Satan to buffet me, lest I should be exalted above measure. For this thing I besought the Lord thrice, that it might depart from me. And he said unto me, My grace is sufficient for thee: for my strength is made perfect in weakness. Most gladly therefore will I rather glory in my infirmities, that the power of Christ may rest upon me.

2 CORINTHIANS 12:7–9

Healing Faith

And he said unto her, Daughter, be of good comfort:
thy faith hath made thee whole; go in peace.

LUKE 8:48

Some physical challenges I don't understand, oh great Physician. I become worried because I can't figure out what is happening. The problems prevent me from being the wife and mother I desire to be because I'm frightened and in pain. I am powerless to resolve the situation, but You are not. Often the only thing preventing healing is my lack of faith. Forgive me, Lord, and heal me.

God Rested

And on the seventh day God ended his work which he had made;
and he rested on the seventh day from all his work which he had made.
GENESIS 2:2

There is truth in the statement that a mother's work is never done. I believe I would be able to fill twenty-four hours, seven days a week, with no effort, but that's not how You planned it, Lord. Even You took time to rest. I can't expect to do my best without taking time to sleep. It's not always easy—I'm rarely caught up. But help me to remember that if You took time out to rest, I surely can't do without it.

Smiles or Broken Hearts

A merry heart maketh a cheerful countenance:
but by sorrow of the heart the spirit is broken.
PROVERBS 15:13

Father, sometimes my heart is so filled with sorrow I wonder if I'll ever smile again. My chest aches from the lump of grief that is there. I am exhausted by the weight on my shoulders. I try to bear it alone, and the load drags down the corners of my mouth. But You can put the smile back on my lips. You can brighten my countenance. You can restore my mind and body, and You will when I let You.

I Shall See God

For I know that my redeemer liveth, and that he shall stand
at the latter day upon the earth: and though after my skin
worms destroy this body, yet in my flesh shall I see God.
JOB 19:25–26

I'm feeling miserable today, Lord. The children have been sick the last few days, and I'm not getting any sleep. I don't have the time or desire to eat properly, and the strain is really catching up to me. I wonder if I'll be able to go on. I'm thankful for the promise that even though my body is wearing down and will one day be destroyed, I will still stand before You in the flesh.

Wash and Be Clean

And his servants came near, and spake unto him, and said, My father, if the prophet had bid thee do some great thing, wouldest thou not have done it? how much rather then, when he saith to thee, Wash, and be clean?

2 KINGS 5:13

It's easy to be critical of men like Naaman, Lord. I wonder why he felt the need to complain about such an easy method of healing, but at times I am the same way. I could choose to eat properly and exercise regularly and get the right amount of sleep. Instead I make excuses for ignoring these simple solutions for better health. For my sake and that of my family, help me to put them into practice.

Refreshing Music

And it came to pass, when the evil spirit from God was upon Saul, that David took an harp, and played with his hand: so Saul was refreshed, and was well, and the evil spirit departed from him.

1 SAMUEL 16:23

I offer my praise, Lord, for the refreshment I find in godly music. At times I feel the chaos of the moment will lead to my collapse. My day is overcrowded, yet my children want more activities. My husband's requests are easy to meet on a normal day, but today I feel as if my head will explode. Thank You for beautiful music to soothe my soul.

Prayer and Healing

And the prayer of faith shall save the sick, and the Lord shall raise him up; and if he have committed sins, they shall be forgiven him.

JAMES 5:15

I try doctors and medication. I try whatever this article or that relative suggests, but real healing comes only when I turn my condition over to You. You just want me to pray. When I pray for my child who is out late, I don't worry. When I pray that my family will escape the virus, I dole out the best immunity. When I release problems to You, You answer prayers.

Thank You, Lord

And [one of the men Jesus healed] fell down on his face at his feet, giving him thanks: and he was a Samaritan.

LUKE 17:16

Dear Jesus, You healed ten lepers, but only one said, "Thank You." How often am I guilty of taking my good health for granted? So many people have health concerns beyond my imagination, yet they thank You for the health they do have. I've tried to teach my children to be thankful for all they have, but at times I'm a poor example. Now I want to say, "Thank You, Lord."

Coming through the Roof

And when they could not come nigh unto him for the press, they uncovered the roof where he was: and when they had broken it up, they let down the bed wherein the sick of the palsy lay.

MARK 2:4

Climbing walls, hanging from the ceiling, going through the roof—You know what it's like in my house, Lord. My children are full of life and energy. It's fun and exciting, but sometimes it can be a bit exhausting. Maybe I will try coming down through the roof myself. I will seek both physical and spiritual uplifting, and You will grant them.

Spiritual Healing First

Bless the LORD, O my soul, and forget not all his benefits:
who forgiveth all thine iniquities; who healeth all thy diseases.

PSALM 103:2–3

It's one of Your greatest themes, dear Jesus. People come to You for physical healing, but the first thing You do is address their spiritual condition. It's not that our health is unimportant. You just want us to have our priorities straight. Lord, let me learn from Your example. My children have many needs that I must attempt to meet, but the greatest of these is spiritual. I will pray for and with them, and we'll study Your Word together.

Hezekiah's Petition

I beseech thee, O LORD, remember now how I have walked before
thee in truth and with a perfect heart, and have done that which
is good in thy sight. And Hezekiah wept sore. And it came to pass,
afore Isaiah was gone out into the middle court, that the word of
the LORD came to him, saying, Turn again, and tell Hezekiah the
captain of my people, Thus saith the LORD, the God of David thy father,
I have heard thy prayer, I have seen thy tears: behold, I will heal thee:
on the third day thou shalt go up unto the house of the LORD.

2 KINGS 20:3–5

I Belong to God

*What? know ye not that your body is the temple of the Holy Ghost
which is in you, which ye have of God, and ye are not your own?
For ye are bought with a price: therefore glorify God in your body,
and in your spirit, which are God's.*

1 CORINTHIANS 6:19–20

It doesn't come as a surprise that I don't belong to me, Lord.
I am Yours, paid for by Your precious blood. Sometimes I
forget though. During pregnancy I was always careful to
eat properly. I tried to avoid caffeine. I exercised but didn't
overdo it. I knew I didn't belong to me. That's what I should
do now. I am Yours, and even how I care for myself can be a
reflection to others of You.

My Joy

The Power of Fellowship with God

And these things write we unto you,
that your joy may be full.
1 John 1:4

We've all seen it—perhaps even worn it. They call it the glow of motherhood. It's that "I can't hide the happy news" look that surrounds an expectant mother. It's a perpetual smile, a lighter step despite her thickening waistline. She is in her glory. The nausea, strange cravings, and moodiness are offset by the thrill that she is about to become a mother. She really hasn't considered that sleepless nights, blown-out diapers, and a drastically altered schedule are just around the corner. She has not yet experienced a three-year-old's temper tantrum, a seven-year-old's broken arm, a ten-year-old's struggle with math, or a teenager's bad decision. She hasn't yet wiped the tears of her adult child who is in the midst of a job loss or a failed marriage.

To the expectant mother, life is pure bliss. She takes the rough mornings, the bulging abdomen, and the swollen ankles in stride because she knows the joy to come is greater than the present difficulty. She imagines that first precious smile she hopes to capture on video camera. She envisions the first birthday and the icing-covered face whose image will eventually make its way into a cherished scrapbook. She thinks of the proud tears she will wipe away as she puts her child on the bus that first day of kindergarten. She sees a bright future for herself and her child. She is optimistic. She is full of joy.

We can look at her cynically and say, "Just wait until you experience. . ." and fill in the blank. Or we can learn from her. We can accept that although our circumstances at times contribute to our happiness, our joy is not dependent upon them.

Nehemiah 12:43 says, "Also that day they offered great sacrifices, and rejoiced: for God had made them rejoice with great joy." Were the Israelites rejoicing because every day was happy? No. Were they living easy lives? Absolutely not! They'd been in captivity. Their beloved temple had been destroyed, and they'd faced terrible opposition as they tried to rebuild it. Worst of all, there was sin among them. From a worldly perspective, they had little to bring them joy. Yet when they repented of their sin, God caused them to rejoice.

Our joy comes from God. Never lose sight of this. Even when your days are pleasant, when your children are well behaved and no one is ill, when all is right with your career, God is the source of true joy. As long as we walk faithfully with Him, we will find reasons to rejoice. His Word is full of descriptions of how to experience this wonderful blessing. Get to know these passages. You will be rewarded more richly than you have ever imagined.

I Will Rejoice

*And ye now therefore have sorrow: but I will see you again,
and your heart shall rejoice, and your joy no man taketh from you.*

JOHN 16:22

You are with me, dear Jesus. What more could I wish? Just being with You today makes my heart sing, and it's a joy no one can steal from me. You have given it freely, and You want it to be mine. I cherish this treasure, and I want those around me to experience it too. Let my life so exude Your joy that my husband, my children, and everyone I meet will desire You also.

Tidings of Great Joy

*And the angel said unto them, Fear not: for, behold, I bring
you good tidings of great joy, which shall be to all people.*

LUKE 2:10

Dear God, You remember how it was when I found out that I was expecting. I couldn't wait to share the news with everyone. Then when the baby arrived, I was filled with tremendous joy, and everyone celebrated with me. Yet this glorious event in my life can't begin to compare with the joyful tidings proclaimed by the angels the night Your Son was born. It is Your Son who makes my life worth living!

In Your Presence Is Joy

*I have set the LORD always before me: because he is at my right
hand, I shall not be moved. Therefore my heart is glad, and my glory
rejoiceth: my flesh also shall rest in hope. For thou wilt not leave
my soul in hell; neither wilt thou suffer thine Holy One to see
corruption. Thou wilt shew me the path of life: in thy presence is
fulness of joy; at thy right hand there are pleasures for evermore.*

PSALM 16:8–11

The Joy of the Lord Is My Strength

For the joy of the LORD is your strength.

NEHEMIAH 8:10

I'm tired today, dear God. There have been moments when I thought I couldn't take another step. The truth is that I can't move forward without You. But You are with me. Your yoke is easy; Your burden is light. You want to take the pressure off me. What a joy it is for me to walk with You—to draw strength from You. What a wondrous gift to be in Your company.

An Obvious Command

Rejoice evermore.

1 THESSALONIANS 5:16

You really can't make it any clearer than this, can You, Lord? Forgive me, please. I'm often guilty of attaching addendums to this command. "Rejoice evermore. . .if the kids clean their rooms and eat their vegetables." "Rejoice evermore. . .if the electric bill doesn't increase, I don't lose my keys, and no one is ill." I'm wrong, Lord. I've no business adding to Your perfect Word. You simply said, "Rejoice evermore." Period.

A Joyful Prayer

And Hannah prayed, and said, My heart rejoiceth in the LORD, mine horn is exalted in the LORD: my mouth is enlarged over mine enemies; because I rejoice in thy salvation. There is none holy as the LORD: for there is none beside thee: neither is there any rock like our God. . . . They that were full have hired out themselves for bread; and they that were hungry ceased: so that the barren hath born seven; and she that hath many children is waxed feeble.

1 SAMUEL 2:1–2, 5

Painful Joy

Behold, happy is the man whom God correcteth:
therefore despise not thou the chastening of the Almighty.
JOB 5:17

My children dislike discipline, Father, but I correct them so their futures can be brighter. I have to admit, I'm not fond of being chastened either, but I know You sometimes need to discipline me to make me useful for You. Oh, how it hurts at times, but what a happy day it will be when You say to me, "Well done, my faithful daughter!"

Fruit of the Spirit

But the fruit of the Spirit is love, joy, peace, longsuffering, gentleness,
goodness, faith, meekness, temperance: against such there is no law.
GALATIANS 5:22–23

I don't see how I could be Your child and not have joy in my life, dear God. Oh, I know I'm still subject to human emotions and problems, but You are at work in my soul. You will cultivate joy within me if I will let You. Then others will see it. My family, my friends—everyone will want You to be their Gardener too. Please let the soil of my heart be fertile for the seeds You want to sow.

My Heart Rejoices

My soul doth magnify the Lord, and my spirit hath rejoiced in God
my Saviour. For he hath regarded the low estate of his handmaiden:
for, behold, from henceforth all generations shall call me blessed. For
he that is mighty hath done to me great things; and holy is his name.
And his mercy is on them that fear him from generation to generation.
LUKE 1:46–50

My Son Has Come Home

For this my son was dead, and is alive again; he was lost,
and is found. And they began to be merry.

LUKE 15:24

It's not easy to watch my child make mistakes, dear Father. I'm sure no one understands that better than You. I've messed up so many times, yet when I repent, You eagerly open Your arms and lovingly welcome me back. I guess that must be why I am able to joyfully embrace my son when he seeks forgiveness. I have had the best example in You.

God Gives Joy

For God giveth to a man that is good in
his sight wisdom, and knowledge, and joy.

ECCLESIASTES 2:26

Oh Giver of all things good, how grateful I am that You have granted me godly happiness. I am truly undeserving of this blessing, but what refreshment it is to turn from the cares of everyday life and to be bathed in Your eternal joy! I am humbled when I recall how willingly You gave of Yourself that I might experience this pleasure.

Restore Your Joy

Make me to hear joy and gladness; that the bones which thou hast
broken may rejoice. Hide thy face from my sins, and blot out all
mine iniquities. Create in me a clean heart, O God; and renew a
right spirit within me. Cast me not away from thy presence; and
take not thy holy spirit from me. Restore unto me the joy of thy
salvation; and uphold me with thy free spirit. Then will I teach
transgressors thy ways; and sinners shall be converted unto thee.

PSALM 51:8–13

Sing with Gladness

Therefore the redeemed of the LORD shall return, and come with singing unto Zion; and everlasting joy shall be upon their head: they shall obtain gladness and joy; and sorrow and mourning shall flee away.

ISAIAH 51:11

Blessed Redeemer, my heart is filled with rejoicing as I consider Your finished work on Calvary and at the garden tomb. Death and the grave have no claim on me, for in You I have my victory. One day I will leave the trials of this world behind and enter the gates of heaven. Oh, what a day that will be! And what joy to know my children will join me as we meet loved ones who've gone before us. A great day is coming!

Joy in God's Word

These things have I spoken unto you, that my joy might remain in you, and that your joy might be full.

JOHN 15:11

You are my guide and instructor, dear God. I do not need to figure out how to live. Your precious Word tells me. It provides the insight I need to be a godly wife and to bring up my children in a manner that pleases You. You teach me how to serve You and to minister to others. You've given everything I need to live an abundant life, and You did it so my joy would be full. How glad I am to have a personal God.

The Power of Complete Trust in God

Nicole was a young woman fully dedicated to Jesus. Her desire was to serve Him no matter what the cost, and that is how she and her husband became part of their college's traveling music ministry. On their way to a meeting, a much larger vehicle struck their van, and the whole group died instantly. It was a devastating time for many, but at Nicole's memorial service, her father made this statement: "We want you to know that we. . .are rejoicing because we know God makes no mistakes."

Wow! A statement like that can come only from a deep relationship with a heavenly Father who grants a peace that passes all understanding. *God makes no mistakes!* These young people were fully serving God, yet this same God allowed their lives to end abruptly. It seems ironic—even unfair—to us, but God sees the bigger picture. Accepting His sovereignty is what allows us to have peace even during times of great difficulty.

Yes, this wonderful woman probably would have continued to reach people for Christ, but we may never know how many lives she will have touched or how many souls will have accepted Christ as a result of the legacy she left and the blessed peace her family exhibited during what seemed a terrible tragedy.

God often works in unusual ways. We will not always comprehend what He is doing, and that is the beauty of the peace He offers. When our trust is fully in Him, and our friends and neighbors see what He does in our lives through both the good times and the bad, I can think of no greater testament to His love.

Are you resting in God's peace today, or are you fighting against or wallowing in the struggles of life? If you are trying to handle challenges alone, it is time to stop. Give them to God, who wants to bathe you in a peace only He can give.

Perfect Peace

Thou wilt keep him in perfect peace, whose mind
is stayed on thee: because he trusteth in thee.

ISAIAH 26:3

This is a passage I want my children to memorize. Such a promise and a challenge are packed into this nugget of scripture. You want us to fill our souls with peace in spite of the terrors around us. If our focus is on You and Your omnipotence, we will trust You. You can envelop us in Your peace. What an amazing God You are!

Peace in the Lord

Hear me when I call, O God of my righteousness: thou hast enlarged
me when I was in distress; have mercy upon me, and hear my
prayer. . . . There be many that say, Who will shew us any good?
LORD, lift thou up the light of thy countenance upon us. Thou hast
put gladness in my heart, more than in the time that their corn
and their wine increased. I will both lay me down in peace,
and sleep: for thou, LORD, only makest me dwell in safety.

PSALM 4:1, 6–8

The Quietness of God

When he giveth quietness, who then can make trouble?

JOB 34:29

We witnessed an unbelievable storm last night. The first crash of thunder brought the children running. We talked about many aspects of the powerful storm. Soon they were excited rather than frightened, and their childish play escalated to new heights. Between their squeals and the storm, things were noisy. Suddenly the power ceased. Slowly the children crept to me, and I softly told the story of the time You calmed the storm. Their breathing slowed; they slept. Your peace filled our home in the midst of the storm.

The Peace of My Children

And all thy children shall be taught of the LORD;
and great shall be the peace of thy children.

ISAIAH 54:13

I'm so glad You want to teach my children, Lord. There is no teacher greater than You. When they learn from You, they will discover all they need to know about the world and the people around them. They will have no reason to fear, for they will have received their instruction from the Master. I dedicate myself to helping my children discover the lessons You have for them so they can be at peace.

To Be Spiritually Minded

For to be carnally minded is death;
but to be spiritually minded is life and peace.

ROMANS 8:6

I've seen both sides of the mind's coin, Jesus. Before You saved me, I was drawn to sinful pleasures. They left me empty. After I accepted You and began to focus on godly things, I discovered new peace. This is what I want for my children. Although only You can save them, I can commit to protecting them from wickedness and surrounding them with purity as much as possible, and I ask You to make them spiritually minded.

Peaceable Wisdom

But the wisdom that is from above is first pure, then peaceable,
gentle, and easy to be intreated, full of mercy and good fruits,
without partiality, and without hypocrisy.

JAMES 3:17

Many people claim their wisdom is from their god, but it seems that much of what they believe is evil. Thank You, Father, that Your wisdom is abundantly good. It brings joy and peace to my heart, but it extends even further. When I apply Your wisdom to the decisions I make, it affects my family and others around me. It can contribute to their peace too. Please give me this wisdom.

Live in Peace

Finally, brethren, farewell. Be perfect, be of good comfort, be of one mind,
live in peace; and the God of love and peace shall be with you.

2 CORINTHIANS 13:11

We have a houseful of people with different personalities, ideas, and attitudes, dear God. Sometimes that can be a lot of fun, but it can also be confusing. Still, You've commanded us to live in peace, and of course, that's what we want too. Please give us the ability to work together. Show us when we should compromise. Fill our home with love and peace.

Getting Along

If it be possible, as much as lieth in you,
live peaceably with all men.
ROMANS 12:18

I'm always trying to teach my children to work out their differences with others in a peaceful, positive way. I know that to reinforce these lessons, I must do my best to live them. I realize it isn't always possible; some people thrive on being difficult. With Your help I will always try to work with those whose opinions differ from mine. I will try to find a suitable solution in each situation.

Hope, Joy, and Peace

Now the God of hope fill you with all joy and peace in believing,
that ye may abound in hope, through the power of the Holy Ghost.
ROMANS 15:13

We just celebrated my son's birthday, dear God. He was thrilled with the presents he received, and we were happy to see his excitement. Still, there is no way the best we could offer can compare to the perfect hope, joy, and peace You give through the Holy Spirit. These are lasting gifts that will bless our lives forever. Let us receive them gladly.

The Holy Ghost, My Comforter

These things have I spoken unto you, being yet present with you. But
the Comforter, which is the Holy Ghost, whom the Father will send
in my name, he shall teach you all things, and bring all things to your
remembrance, whatsoever I have said unto you. Peace I leave with you, my
peace I give unto you: not as the world giveth, give I unto you. Let not your
heart be troubled, neither let it be afraid. Ye have heard how I said unto
you, I go away, and come again unto you. If ye loved me, ye would rejoice,
because I said, I go unto the Father: for my Father is greater than I.
JOHN 14:25–28

Paths of Peace

Her ways are ways of pleasantness, and all her paths are peace.
PROVERBS 3:17

All-knowing God, I realize Proverbs 3:17 is describing wisdom, but I would love for those words to describe me too. A significant amount of peace is needed to bring up children. I need to be able to handle the necessary discipline with a calm spirit. I need to help my children resolve their differences in a positive way. I need to handle the pressures of daily life with a serenity that comes from You. Lord, make my paths peaceable.

Perfection and Peace

Mark the perfect man, and behold the upright:
for the end of that man is peace.
PSALM 37:37

Everyone wants to experience peace, Lord. I'll admit I've tried more than one method of obtaining it. It's obvious that human attempts are limited at best. But You've made it clear that perfection leads to peace. "Impossible," many will say, but You aren't saying we'll never make mistakes. You're simply saying that if we walk according to Your Word and sincerely grow in faith, Your peace will result.

Strength and Peace

The LORD will give strength unto his people;
the LORD will bless his people with peace.

PSALM 29:11

It's interesting the way You couple strength and peace. It almost seems as if they don't go together. Still, I am reminded of my husband as he plays with our children. He's strong and could easily hurt them, but he loves them and keeps his strength under control. They feel safe and loved and at peace. That's how we feel in Your presence, Lord.

Step Lively Now

For ye shall go out with joy, and be led forth with peace:
the mountains and the hills shall break forth before you into
singing, and all the trees of the field shall clap their hands.

ISAIAH 55:12

I sit here staring out my kitchen window, Lord. My children and their dog are frolicking on the hill nearby. Their laughter fills the air. They are so carefree. I am reminded that when I walk with You, my step will also be lighter. You will take my cares upon You and embrace me with Your peace. The whole world is brighter when You are the center of my life.

The Power of a Sound Mind

It was just a normal workday for the millions of people across this country. Kerri's phone rang, and her husband's voice came over the line: "Did you hear that a plane just crashed into one of the towers of the World Trade Center?" he asked. As they speculated about what had happened, the second plane crashed into the second tower. At that moment they realized it was an act of terrorism. They talked a few minutes more; then Kerri walked to her friend's office. On the way, she heard several coworkers on their phones with friends and family. Soon they were all assembled for a company meeting. It was a somber group that September morning in 2001.

Kerri was seven months pregnant with her first child. As she sat in that large room surrounded by shocked and teary-eyed people, she kept thinking, *What have I done? What kind of world am I bringing this tiny, helpless child into?* It wasn't long after those thoughts that God directed her attention to Proverbs 3:25–26: "Be not afraid of sudden fear, neither of the desolation of the wicked, when it cometh. For the LORD shall be thy confidence, and shall keep thy foot from being taken." That passage grabbed her so strongly that next to it, in the margin of her Bible, she wrote "9/11/01."

Those words sustained her many times after that tragic day. She knew that in a world full of sin and its effects, there would be plenty to fear in life. She wouldn't let fear consume her though, because "greater is he that is in you, than he that is in the world" (1 John 4:4).

Make this verse personal. If Christ is your Savior, He is in *you*! Circle that little word "you" and put your name beside it.

We can use fear in a positive way. It can motivate us to do something about the problem. While it's true there was nothing Kerri could do to stop the 9/11 terrorist attacks or change the world into which her son would soon be born, she could reevaluate her own walk with the Lord. She could dedicate herself to being a godly mother and training her child to know and love God. Sure, the bad stuff didn't disappear, but when she learned to apply Romans 8:28 to her life, she gave her fears to God, and He sustained her.

Mercy and Fear

And his mercy is on them that fear him
from generation to generation.

LUKE 1:50

I've learned that fear is a great tool if it doesn't consume me. Just yesterday I worked at instilling in my young daughter a respectful fear of the hot stove. She knows good things come from those pans on the burners, but she also knows she must respect the stove or she will suffer.

Similarly, I know You are an awesome God. I'll be blessed if I respect You. If I take You lightly, I'll pay the consequences.

Sin Leads to Fear

And he said, I heard thy voice in the garden, and I was afraid,
because I was naked; and I hid myself.

GENESIS 3:10

"Don't tell Mommy." I hear that often. Unfortunately, Lord, You've probably heard something similar from my lips. It seems I fear the consequences of sin more than I hate the evil itself. Like my children, I pretend that if I cover it up, You won't know it exists. Still, there's that gnawing fear of discovery. I know although my kids sometimes pull it off with me, I'll never get away with hiding sin from You. Keep me from evil, Lord.

The Courage of a Lion

The wicked flee when no man pursueth:
but the righteous are bold as a lion.

PROVERBS 28:1

Father, You've created many beautiful creatures. As a family we love to visit zoos and watch nature programs. The children even pretend to be animals. I'm always amazed by the lions. It seems the big cats fear nothing. Why? Because that's how they are designed. It's the courage I can have when I'm walking with You, because You are on my side. Lord, make me bold as a lion.

Whom Shall I Fear?

The LORD is my light and my salvation; whom shall I fear?
the LORD is the strength of my life; of whom shall I be afraid?
PSALM 27:1

My children, like so many others, are fearful of the dark, dear Lord. If I add a night-light to their room, all fear vanishes. God, I would do well to be afraid if I had to make my way through this sin-darkened world without You, but I don't. You are my light and my salvation. Because You are by my side, I have no reason to be afraid.

God Fights My Battles

Hear, O Israel, ye approach this day unto battle against your enemies:
let not your hearts faint, fear not, and do not tremble, neither be ye
terrified because of them; for the LORD your God is he that goeth with
you, to fight for you against your enemies, to save you.
DEUTERONOMY 20:3–4

Lord, I am determined to take a stand for You. There will be those who oppose me, and I will have battles to fight. My neighbor might be upset when I don't join his sinful parties. There could be trouble with my child's teacher who doesn't understand my convictions. Unfortunately, there might even be times when another Christian will wish to do battle. I will not fear. It is You who will fight for me.

No Fear in Love

There is no fear in love; but perfect love casteth out fear:
because fear hath torment. He that feareth is not made perfect in love.

1 John 4:18

Sometimes when I think of the future, I am frightened for my children. What if they turn from You, Lord? What if they become involved in sin? Then I remember that dwelling on these possibilities won't help matters. What I need to do is shower my children with godly love and spend much time praying for them. After all, they are in Your hands.

My God Reigns

Say to them that are of a fearful heart, Be strong, fear not:
behold, your God will come with vengeance, even God
with a recompence; he will come and save you.

Isaiah 35:4

Father, I'll always remember my trip to Colorado Springs several years ago. We visited a very unique place called Gog and Magog. It was so desolate, so eerie. It reminded me of the sinful condition of this world. But all around me, I could see the indescribable beauty of the mountains. Like Gog and Magog, my journey on earth can be daunting, but when Your kingdom is established, all will be beautiful.

Save Me, Lord

For I have heard the slander of many: fear was on every side:
while they took counsel together against me, they devised to take
away my life. But I trusted in thee, O LORD: I said, Thou art my
God. My times are in thy hand: deliver me from the hand of
mine enemies, and from them that persecute me. Make thy face
to shine upon thy servant: save me for thy mercies' sake.

Psalm 31:13–16

Depart from Evil

Be not wise in thine own eyes: fear the LORD, and depart from evil.
PROVERBS 3:7

My arrogance gets me into trouble sometimes. I enter into situations I think I'm strong enough to handle, and I forget to seek Your direction, Father. Then I stumble. I hurt myself and others just because I don't fear You as much as I should. Instead of fleeing evil, I walk right into its path. Forgive me, Lord. Change my attitude. Help me to walk according to Your wisdom.

Speak the Word with Boldness

And now, Lord, behold their threatenings: and grant unto thy servants, that with all boldness they may speak thy word.
ACTS 4:29

Teacher-led prayer has been exiled from schools. Some people want Your name removed from national landmarks. In some areas of the world, any mention of You is forbidden. So many Christians give in to the threats. Oh Lord, grant me boldness. I want to do my part to win souls for Your kingdom. I want my children to understand Your truths, and I want them to grow up courageously proclaiming Your name.

Redemption Draweth Nigh

Men's hearts failing them for fear, and for looking after those things
which are coming on the earth: for the powers of heaven shall be
shaken. . . . And when these things begin to come to pass, then look up,
and lift up your heads; for your redemption draweth nigh.

LUKE 21:26, 28

Every day I open the newspaper to discover more stories of murder, drug abuse, child abuse, and a host of other horrible situations. I didn't used to think about them much. They happened in other cities, not here. It's not so anymore. Now I consider how these problems could affect my family. I shouldn't worry though. I'll try to protect my children from harm and horror, but I'll also rejoice, knowing that You're coming soon.

Don't Anger God

And the anger of the LORD was kindled against Moses, and he said,
Is not Aaron the Levite thy brother? I know that he can
speak well. And also, behold, he cometh forth to meet thee:
and when he seeth thee, he will be glad in his heart.

EXODUS 4:14

Most powerful God, how many times have I caused You anger because I was afraid to do what You told me? How many opportunities have I missed because I let fear control me instead of letting You be in charge? Lord, I know that if You tell me to do something, You will empower me. Give me courage to do what's right. I don't want to cause Your wrath, and I don't want to miss Your blessing.

Fast and Pray

Go, gather together all the Jews that are present in Shushan,
and fast ye for me, and neither eat nor drink three days, night or day:
I also and my maidens will fast likewise; and so will I go in unto the
king, which is not according to the law: and if I perish, I perish.

ESTHER 4:16

God, it seems ironic that Esther's task involved risking her life in order to beg that it be spared. It's no wonder she balked at first. Yet she realized how important this was to her people. Many people were fasting and praying for her, and what a miracle was born! At times I too face fearsome duties. Rather than fleeing them, I will fast and pray and place the situation in Your hands.

Prayer of the Sheep

The LORD is my shepherd; I shall not want. He maketh me to lie down in
green pastures: he leadeth me beside the still waters. He restoreth my soul:
he leadeth me in the paths of righteousness for his name's sake. Yea, though
I walk through the valley of the shadow of death, I will fear no evil: for
thou art with me; thy rod and thy staff they comfort me. Thou preparest a
table before me in the presence of mine enemies: thou anointest my head
with oil; my cup runneth over. Surely goodness and mercy shall follow me
all the days of my life: and I will dwell in the house of the LORD for ever.

PSALM 23

My Purpose

The Power of Positive Influence

What is your purpose in life? Perhaps you are so busy fulfilling that purpose that you've never really given it much thought, but God has a perfect plan for each one of us. Some things He is very specific about. For instance, we are to praise God (Psalm 150:6). We are to worship God (Matthew 4:10). We are commanded to witness (Acts 1:8). As mothers we are to raise our children in a godly environment (Ephesians 6:4). I realize Paul is speaking to fathers here, but as moms, we need to do our part too.

There are just some things that we as believers know we are to do. It's important to be faithful in these areas, because when we are, God is able to begin revealing what He has for us to do personally.

Did you realize that God set His purpose for you in place before you were even born (Jeremiah 1:5)? To some people that might seem a bit presumptuous. We like to be independent and free to make our own decisions. We need to remember that God created us. He knows us better than we know ourselves. Based on what He knows about us and the world around us, He designed a plan for each of us. We do have a choice to make. We must decide whether we will discover and fulfill God's purpose, thus attaining abundant joy, satisfaction, and eternal reward, or whether we will stumble about trying to do our own thing.

There are many different things we can do to glorify God, but if I'm upset because I think your duties are more glamorous than mine, I am not going to accomplish anything worthwhile. God did not plan for all of us to do the same thing (1 Corinthians 12), but each of us working together and doing our part for the Lord is what will draw people to Him.

As mothers we should set an example of faithfulness for our children to follow. Just as God has a plan for us, He has one for our kids. If they see us obeying God, they are more likely to do the same themselves. What if Zacharias and Elisabeth had refused to obey God? Would their son, John the Baptist, have been willing to live such a wild and rugged life and point so many to the Savior? Only God knows the answer, but the question is worth considering. Won't you ask God to show you what your purpose is and to help you fulfill it? Be faithful. As you are, He will reveal more and more of His plan for you.

Loving God

He that loveth father or mother more than me is not worthy of me:
and he that loveth son or daughter more than me is not worthy of me.
MATTHEW 10:37

Oh God, one of my favorite times of day is when my young daughter awakens. I go into her room, and she stands there reaching for me with the most beautiful smile. I feel her love immediately. While I'm glad my child delights in me, it is infinitely more important that she learns to love You. Help me to point her in that direction.

My Wages

And in the same house remain, eating and drinking such things as they
give: for the labourer is worthy of his hire. Go not from house to house.
LUKE 10:7

Motherhood has aptly been called a "labor of love." The financial benefits may not exist, but the dividends of the occupation cannot be matched. I have the opportunity to teach my children that You love them. I get to be a part of their acceptance of You. You allow me to aid them in their spiritual growth and understanding. As I watch them develop into young people who honor You, I realize the compensation of my life's work is beyond compare.

Made to Praise the Lord

All thy works shall praise thee, O LORD; and thy saints shall bless thee.
They shall speak of the glory of thy kingdom, and talk of thy power;
to make known to the sons of men his mighty acts, and the glorious
majesty of his kingdom. Thy kingdom is an everlasting kingdom, and thy
dominion endureth throughout all generations. The LORD upholdeth all
that fall, and raiseth up all those that be bowed down. The eyes of all
wait upon thee; and thou givest them their meat in due season.
PSALM 145:10–15

Created for a Purpose

For by him were all things created, that are in heaven, and that are in earth, visible and invisible, whether they be thrones, or dominions, or principalities, or powers: all things were created by him, and for him.

COLOSSIANS 1:16

Dear Creator of all things, when You spoke this world into existence, when You formed me with Your hands, they weren't just random acts of Your power. All creation, including me, is intended to glorify and praise You. I need to convey this message to my children. They need to understand that they too are here to honor You. Together we can exalt Your name.

God's Instructions

And God blessed them, and God said unto them, Be fruitful, and multiply, and replenish the earth, and subdue it: and have dominion over the fish of the sea, and over the fowl of the air, and over every living thing that moveth upon the earth.

GENESIS 1:28

From the earliest days of creation, You have been specific about what You want us to do, Lord. You said You want me to care for the earth in a way that pleases You. You want me to bring children into the world who also will help care for it. I am to learn what I can about Your creation and to help my children understand it, for it is indeed amazing.

Glorify God

Whether therefore ye eat, or drink, or whatsoever ye do, do all to the glory of God.

1 CORINTHIANS 10:31

I've read this passage too many times to count, Lord, but I really needed it this morning. My daughter's class is going on a field trip. She begged me to go as a chaperone, but I couldn't take off work to do it. I feel angry that my job sometimes prevents me from being where I want to be, but You know best. You've given me my job, and I need to honor You by doing my best. Please make my attitude right.

The Results of the Rod of Reproof

The rod and reproof give wisdom: but a child left to himself bringeth his mother to shame.

PROVERBS 29:15

My children have big ideas, Lord. They want to do things their own way. I know that leaving them to their own designs could be quite disastrous, but that doesn't mean I enjoy the discipline. Still, I know that to develop wisdom and responsibility, they need to be corrected while they are young. Please give me the direction I need to guide them into becoming properly independent.

A Shining Light

That ye may be blameless and harmless, the sons of God, without rebuke, in the midst of a crooked and perverse nation, among whom ye shine as lights in the world.

PHILIPPIANS 2:15

Light makes me feel good, Father. I love it when the sun comes streaming through my windows. When the day ends, I'm glad to be able to turn on the lights and promote a cheerful atmosphere in my home. Light offers hope. That's what I want to do. I want to draw my children to You. I want my friends and neighbors and even people I don't know to see You in me. Let me be a light for You, Father.

My Testimony

Having your conversation honest among the Gentiles: that, whereas
they speak against you as evildoers, they may by your good works,
which they shall behold, glorify God in the day of visitation.

1 PETER 2:12

Father, by Your grace You saved me. My life is not what it
was at the beginning. Salvation is a grand gift, but You don't
want me to keep it to myself. You always planned for me to
share it. Many people won't want it. They'll look for evidence
in my life to discredit all I say. Help me to live in such a way
that they won't find anything. My purpose is to draw them to
You. Let my life and speech do just that.

When Others Are in Charge

Let as many servants as are under the yoke count their
own masters worthy of all honour, that the name
of God and his doctrine be not blasphemed.

1 TIMOTHY 6:1

Last night when I told my son to clean his room, his lower lip
shot out. "This is not fun," he complained. "Maybe not, but
it's a job that needs done," I replied. I thought about the way
my boss sometimes asks me to do jobs that aren't fun. I could
complain and blow my testimony, but I know I should just do
the work cheerfully, realizing that it's helpful to someone else.
In this way I will bring glory to You.

Be Holy

Speak unto all the congregation of the children of Israel,
and say unto them, Ye shall be holy: for I the LORD your God am holy.

LEVITICUS 19:2

Dear God, I don't know how many times I have said to my children, "Do this." They say, "Why?" I flippantly respond, "Because I said so." In reality I should be setting the example. You've told me to be perfect because You're perfect. My children need to understand that I don't have double standards. I will determine to be a positive influence.

His Mother Taught Him

The words of king Lemuel, the prophecy
that his mother taught him.
PROVERBS 31:1

I can appreciate these writings of Lemuel, dear God. Here's a grown man—a king—and he readily admits that something his mother taught him had value. I want to be available to guide my grown children, but they don't seem interested in my advice. Help me to handle situations properly so that they know I love them and that I'm not trying to nag. Although they won't always follow my suggestions, help me to trust that they'll follow You.

Sleep as a Reward

The sleep of a labouring man is sweet, whether he eat little or much:
but the abundance of the rich will not suffer him to sleep.
ECCLESIASTES 5:12

It was a busy day, Lord, and truthfully I'm exhausted, but I feel great. This morning my toddler joined me in window washing. It took extra time with her in tow, but what a blast! When my older children arrived home from school, we worked in the garden and enjoyed some of the results for supper. What a day! You intend for me to work hard. Now I know I'll get a good night's sleep.

A Woman Who Fears the Lord

Favour is deceitful, and beauty is vain: but a woman
that feareth the LORD, she shall be praised.

PROVERBS 31:30

Father, there are many material things to tempt me. At times I'm drawn to them. And society tells me that to be truly successful, I must be beautiful. Of course, it also offers all the products I need to accomplish that. I know there's nothing wrong with being attractive, but the reason You put me here is to fear and honor You. Real beauty and success lie in my desire to glorify You.

The Power of Good Stewardship

Rhonda planned, organized, and held a garage sale. She made a decent amount of money that she intended to use as her Christmas fund. Soon after, she learned her church was having a special offering for a family in need. Rhonda and her husband prayed about how much to give. In a last-minute decision, she placed all of the garage sale money in the offering.

A short time later, Rhonda was involved in an automobile accident. She wasn't injured, but her vehicle needed repaired. She received some estimates, and the insurance check was issued. In the end the repairs cost far less than originally thought, and she was able to keep the extra money—an amount far in excess of the amount given in that special offering.

God does work in amazing ways. Often we don't understand what He is doing, but His ways are perfect. Each of us has a different financial situation. By the world's standards some of us are quite well-to-do. Others struggle to make ends meet; many of us are somewhere in the middle.

God has quite a bit to say about our finances. First of all, whether we are rich or poor, our money belongs to Him. He expects us to be good stewards of what he has given us (Matthew 25:14–30). He also expects us to have the right attitude about money. Matthew 6:19–21 reminds us that laying up treasure in heaven is infinitely more worthwhile than storing up goods on earth.

Do you remember the story of the rich but foolish landowner in Luke 12:16–21? God blessed him abundantly. However, instead of thanking God, the foolish man took all the credit and decided to spend the next several years irresponsibly. He forgot that God was still in control, and God's plans were different. What a shame he squandered God's blessing.

We moms sometimes get preoccupied with our financial situations. We shouldn't though. God has given us plenty of advice in His Word. We just need to spend time talking to Him about it.

Great Riches

There is that maketh himself rich, yet hath nothing:
there is that maketh himself poor, yet hath great riches.

PROVERBS 13:7

Lord, sometimes I'm tempted to envy those with "things." I begin thinking about how much easier life would be if I just made more money. Then I consider what that would involve. We'd share fewer family meals. I'd rarely play games with or read to my children. In fact, someone else would be raising them most of the time. As I look at it that way, I realize what wonderful riches I have.

A Willing Heart

Speak unto the children of Israel, that they bring me
an offering: of every man that giveth it willingly
with his heart ye shall take my offering.

EXODUS 25:2

Make my heart willing, Lord, for it's the only way my gift will be blessed. Our church has asked for financial contributions that really are needed. I intend to give toward the need, but I want to do it out of true desire and not because I feel guilty. Part of me wants to hold back so I can use the money for my children, but I know that when I give to Your work, my children and others will benefit. God, please make my giving pure.

A Changed Heart

And Zacchaeus stood, and said unto the Lord: Behold, Lord, the half of my
goods I give to the poor; and if I have taken any thing from any man by
false accusation, I restore him fourfold. And Jesus said unto him, This day
is salvation come to this house, forsomuch as he also is a son of Abraham.
For the Son of man is come to seek and to save that which was lost.

LUKE 19:8–10

Blessed Be the Name of the Lord

*Naked came I out of my mother's womb, and naked shall
I return thither: the LORD gave, and the LORD hath
taken away; blessed be the name of the LORD.*

JOB 1:21

Father, when Job spoke these words, he'd already faced horrible tragedy, but the worst was yet to come. I am always amazed that even as he begged for an explanation, he never turned his back on You. He realized nothing was really his, so although his losses were painful, he was able to endure.

I know that difficulties are inevitable. You give and take away as You see fit, and I must bless You.

Robbery!

*Will a man rob God? Yet ye have robbed me. But ye say,
Wherein have we robbed thee? In tithes and offerings.*

MALACHI 3:8

Sirens screamed throughout my house. A silver badge flashed briefly as little hands grabbed my wrists. "You're under arrest, Mommy! You robbed the bank!" And I was led away to the bedroom jailhouse. As I pondered the scene, I realized I would never rob a bank or steal from a store. Yet how many times have I robbed You, Lord? When I fail to give tithes and offerings, I rob You. Please forgive me.

Caesar

*Then saith he unto them, Render therefore unto Caesar
the things which are Caesar's; and unto God the things that are God's.*

MATTHEW 22:21

Every time I vote there seems to be some levy on the ballot. Sometimes they are good levies; other times they are questionable. Still, I'm glad I can vote, and when taxes do get passed, I need to take responsibility and pay them. I must set the example for my children and be a good testimony to others. Lord, please help me not to complain, and please provide for our needs.

The Question of Loans

My son, if thou be surety for thy friend, if thou hast stricken thy hand with a stranger, thou art snared with the words of thy mouth, thou art taken with the words of thy mouth.

PROVERBS 6:1–2

Lord, how I want my children to become financially responsible individuals. I'd like to be able to cosign on loans for their first cars or real estate; I'd even like to be able to provide the loan when possible, but I need to know I won't regret it. I need to be sure that the kids are mature enough to make their payments and that my own credit won't be ruined. Please provide the wisdom I need.

The Joy of Giving

Upon the first day of the week let every one of you lay by him in store, as God hath prospered him, that there be no gatherings when I come.

1 CORINTHIANS 16:2

Dear God, it's the holiday season. It looks as though my children will have a nice Christmas, but for some in our church, there might not be gifts under the tree. I'd like to use this opportunity to teach my kids about the joy of giving. Help all of us to remember that as You bless us, we should bless others. And thank You for the greatest gift ever known—Jesus.

Stir My Heart

And they came, every one whose heart stirred him up,
and every one whom his spirit made willing, and they
brought the LORD's offering to the work of the tabernacle of the
congregation, and for all his service, and for the holy garments.

EXODUS 35:21

It's exciting to have some small part in increasing Your kingdom, God. At times it seems hard to let go of that hard-earned extra bit of cash, but what joy when I do! Although I don't always know exactly how that offering will be used when I drop it in the plate at church, I do know that its ultimate purpose will be to bring souls to You. So stir my heart, Father. Make me a willing giver.

More Than Enough

And they spake unto Moses, saying, The people bring much more than
enough for the service of the work, which the LORD commanded to make.

EXODUS 36:5

Oh Lord, has there been a time in recent history that Your people have brought more than enough for Your work? Everything costs so much these days, Father. Updates, repairs, insurance, small supplies—nothing is free, but much is worthwhile. If You'll do a work in our hearts, we Your people will bring more than enough. We'll abundantly offer our time, talents, and finances, and we'll leave a godly heritage for our kids.

Treasure in Heaven

Jesus said unto him, If thou wilt be perfect, go and
sell that thou hast, and give to the poor, and thou shalt
have treasure in heaven: and come and follow me.

MATTHEW 19:21

Good Master, how sad You must have been the day the wealthy young man turned his back on You in favor of his riches. How often do I hurt You by putting "things" before my relationship with You? I don't have great wealth, but at times my attitude isn't much different than this man's. Forgive me, Jesus. I want to follow You fully.

Sowing and Reaping

But this I say, He which soweth sparingly shall reap also sparingly; and he which soweth bountifully shall reap also bountifully.

2 CORINTHIANS 9:6

You know how much the children and I enjoy our garden, Lord. From the smell of freshly tilled soil to the first seedlings and the earliest harvest, each moment is a reward in its own right. How exciting too to see missionaries on the field, kids saved through children's ministries, and outreach programs begun, and to know I had a part through my prayers and finances. As we abundantly sow our garden, let us also abundantly sow seeds for Your harvest.

Be Content

Let your conversation be without covetousness; and be content with such things as ye have: for he hath said, I will never leave thee, nor forsake thee.

HEBREWS 13:5

I don't understand, Lord. The people next door just built a huge addition, and they only have one child! Our small house is crowded, but we can't afford to add on. I'm tempted to complain, but then I remember that You live here with us too. You'll never leave us, and You don't complain about tight spaces. You help us, and You let us enjoy each other in our cozy little home.

God Meets My Needs

But my God shall supply all your need
according to his riches in glory by Christ Jesus.
PHILIPPIANS 4:19

Sometimes I have a hard time helping my children differentiate between needs and wants. They say, "It's hot; we need to go swimming." I say, "You want to go swimming, but playing under those shade trees will help cool you off too." Do You smile when this happens, remembering how I just said, "I need a new dishwasher," when a bottle of detergent and a dishrag would work? Father, I know You truly will provide for my needs. Thank You.

The Power of a Willing Heart

There is no doubt that God expects us to willingly serve Him and others. It seems though that there is a fine line between what is good and what is too much. Certainly God wants us to attend church and share the Gospel with others. There is an area in our churches for each of us to work. Service also can extend to participating in a community project or meeting a neighbor's need. It includes being a friend and offering a listening ear. Many types of ministry and service bring glory to God. They might involve time, money, or sacrifice, but being a blessing to others is worth it.

There is such a thing as doing too much though. Serving others while ignoring the needs of your husband and children can have damaging effects. I have known people who were so busy with their commitments that they virtually lost their kids. This is not what God intended. Remember our discussion in chapter 12 about stewardship? God has given us stewardship of His children, and He expects us to apply His wisdom in our relationship with them. If we lose our kids, how can we expect Him to bless our other efforts?

The area of service requires much prayer. We need to ask God where He wants us to volunteer, and we need to ask for strength and stamina to do all things well. Christ, our best example, came to be a servant, but even He took time to rest and to spend time with those closest to Him.

He also involved His disciples in His work. So when we're considering what we might do, why not think about ways we can involve our families? If you volunteer to clean your church, take the kids along to help, and stop for ice cream afterward. If there's a need for Sunday school teachers, find a class you and your husband can co-teach. God loves a willing heart. How much more must a willing family please Him?

Muddy Feet

If I then, your Lord and Master, have washed your feet;
ye also ought to wash one another's feet.

JOHN 13:14

Recently we have had a good deal of rain, and the children have been thoroughly enjoying the mud. It's been a blast to watch them, but it's made for some very filthy kids. As I scrubbed the mud from between my son's toes, I thought about Your example when You washed the disciples' feet. I want to follow Your lead. I want to bless my family and others. I only ask for a servant's heart.

Gladness

I was glad when they said unto me,
Let us go into the house of the LORD.

PSALM 122:1

I'm ashamed to admit I don't always feel glad about going to church, Lord. I know I need to go to be encouraged and to be an encouragement, but sometimes I feel as though it's just one more thing on my to-do list. Please give me a better attitude. Restore the gladness that comes from fellowship with other believers. There is so much I can give and gain. Besides, my children need the opportunity. Lord, I will be glad.

Teaching Children to Serve

And the child did minister unto
the LORD before Eli the priest.

1 SAMUEL 2:11

As a mother of small children, I am greatly blessed. I am also extremely busy. There are some tasks I could be teaching my children to perform, but so often it's easier to do them myself. God, I know You are continually working on me to make me a better servant. I cannot refuse to do the same for my little ones. They might balk at it as I often do, but together we'll be works in progress.

Bring Forth Fruit

Herein is my Father glorified, that ye
bear much fruit; so shall ye be my disciples.
JOHN 15:8

We watched and waited, and we were so excited when beans and radishes poked through the earth. We saw onions, peas, and lettuce, and we cheered. But where was the sweet corn? We replanted and waited. Soon we were rewarded. I'm glad we didn't give up. Let us be as diligent as we sow and nurture Gospel seeds. We want to glorify You in the abundance of fruit we bring to You.

Building the Church

And have ye not read this scripture; The stone which the
builders rejected is become the head of the corner?
MARK 12:10

I am privileged to be part of a special building project, and You are the chief cornerstone, dear Jesus. You dwell among this body of believers—Your church—and bless it in innumerable ways. We are a work in progress. We are Your bride, and we will not be complete until You come to take us to heaven. Keep us pure, and let us be a body of believers who will draw others to You.

A Lesson from Dorcas

Now there was at Joppa a certain disciple named Tabitha,
which by interpretation is called Dorcas: this woman was
full of good works and almsdeeds which she did.

ACTS 9:36

Before Dorcas died, she was apparently known only to her
community, but she was loved for her giving heart. She
honored You, and You wanted to use her further, so You raised
her from the dead. She must have been more popular then.
Perhaps people heard what had happened and were saved. I'd
like to be able to claim Philippians 1:24–25 with Dorcas and
Paul. To die is to be with Christ, but to remain on earth is to
be a blessing to others.

Labor of Love

For God is not unrighteous to forget your work and labour
of love, which ye have shewed toward his name, in that
ye have ministered to the saints, and do minister.

HEBREWS 6:10

Sometimes it seems as if being a mother is all labor; other
times it's all love. Usually it's a balance of the two. In any case,
it is very time-consuming. I don't always have the time or
the energy to serve others as I would like to, and I feel guilty.
Yet I am reminded that ministering to my children is a high
calling. You will not overlook it, and You will bless me when
I can help others.

The Proper Attitude

But lay up for yourselves treasures in heaven, where neither moth nor rust
doth corrupt, and where thieves do not break through nor steal.

MATTHEW 6:20

I need wisdom in teaching my children the proper attitude about service, God. I want them to have a healthy amount of pride in their work so they will do their best. At the same time, they need to understand that human praise pales in comparison to the joy that comes from pleasing You. It's a touchy situation. Please give me guidance.

The Courage of a Child

But Peter and John answered and said unto them, Whether it be right in the sight of God to hearken unto you more than unto God, judge ye. For we cannot but speak the things which we have seen and heard.
ACTS 4:19–20

In Sunday school my daughter made a Gospel caterpillar. It consisted of different-colored circles, each representing some aspect of the Christian faith. When she asked for materials to reproduce it at home, I gave them to her, figuring it would entertain her for a while. I had no idea she'd make one for each of her school classmates. "Mommy, they need to know Jesus too," she said. Oh, to have such determination to witness.

Tried by Fire

Every man's work shall be made manifest: for the day shall declare it, because it shall be revealed by fire; and the fire shall try every man's work of what sort it is.
1 CORINTHIANS 3:13

The promise of a trip to the pool put my children in motion. The deal was that their rooms first had to be cleaned to my satisfaction. Fifteen minutes later they returned. My son's room passed easily. While my daughter's floor was clean, the contents were piled onto her bed, and her comforter was draped over them. Her room did not pass. I know You'll try my works too, Lord. Oh, how I want to please You.

Important Jobs

We have many members in one body,
and all members have not the same office.

ROMANS 12:4

Lord, it's amazing how often the lessons I share with my children end up speaking volumes to me. For instance, my son wanted to skip his part of dinner cleanup. I explained that would leave his sister with all the work and less time for fun. Suddenly I thought about the fact that when I ignore my responsibilities at church, someone else has to step in. All jobs are important, and I should take mine seriously too.

With Christ Living in Us

I am crucified with Christ: nevertheless I live; yet not I, but Christ
liveth in me: and the life which I now live in the flesh I live by the
faith of the Son of God, who loved me, and gave himself for me.

GALATIANS 2:20

We've been praying hard for one of our friends to receive You, Lord. We share the Gospel with her, and week after week the children invite her to church. She's just so afraid of what she'll have to give up if she accepts You. Oh Lord, help her to see what she will gain if she does allow You to live within her. Open her eyes so that she'll understand that living with You truly is life.

Required to Be Faithful

Moreover it is required in stewards,
that a man be found faithful.

1 CORINTHIANS 4:2

Master, You've given me stewardship over so many precious gifts—my family, my home, my ministries. You expect me to care for these blessings and serve them faithfully. You put them in my care for a specific reason. They belong to You, and I must treat them that way. Lord, give me the wisdom to carry out the duties You have given me. I so desire to hear You say one day, "Well done, good and faithful servant."

Too Late

The harvest is past, the summer
is ended, and we are not saved.

JEREMIAH 8:20

Yesterday the children and I picked many quarts of strawberries. They thrilled at the sight of their baskets filling with ripe red fruit, but even as we picked, we discovered rotten, mushy berries on the plants or lying on the ground. It was too late to enjoy them. Oh God, how many lives have gone to waste because I waited too long to witness? You've given me a priceless lesson from the overripe berries. Let me never forget it.

The Power of Hope in God

"Thank You that we're going to go swimming," my five-year-old confidently prayed. It was a praise full of faith. The reason being, at that point we had no plans whatsoever of going swimming. He was hopeful though, and he was trusting God to fulfill his desires.

It's easy for us to smile at the innocence of such prayers, but I have a feeling God smiles for a far different reason. The faith of a young child pleases Him. That's why He said if we want to accept Christ, we must become as a little child (Mark 10:15). A young child's faith is so sincere. He hasn't become so full of pride that he believes he can do everything on his own. He places his hope in God and realizes that it's God who meets his needs.

Since becoming a mother, I have learned a lot, and my children have been the ones who have taught me. William Wordsworth said, "The child is the father of the man." In other words, we can learn a lot about life and faith from the precious babes with whom we've been blessed.

You see, had it been me, I probably would have said, "Lord, I'd really like to go swimming today. If it's Your will, please give us that opportunity." There's nothing wrong with that prayer, but it speaks only of possibility. It doesn't show a hope based on a complete trust that God is going to answer my prayer.

We also might be tempted to argue that God really isn't interested in simple things such as whether we go swimming. Why teach or encourage our children to pray about such things? Matthew 10:30 tells us God knows exactly how many hairs are on each one of our heads. If He takes note of such a tiny detail, we have every reason to believe He cares about every area of our lives, from the biggest to the smallest.

Sometimes we're just too proud or embarrassed to accept that truth. We trust Him with our eternal souls and with our big problems or decisions, but we fear He will laugh at us or scold us if we waste time on minor details. That's not how God works though. We start out with a small seed of faith. We begin talking to God about each area of life. The more time we spend with Him, the more our faith grows. We just need to decide to hope in God.

Oh, that we could learn from our children!

And Thy House

And they said, Believe on the Lord Jesus Christ,
and thou shalt be saved, and thy house.

ACTS 16:31

Lord, I understand my children aren't automatically saved simply because I've accepted You, but when I exhibit an unadulterated confidence in You, they are sure to notice it and more likely to trust You than if I had only a casual faith. I've experienced much joy in my walk with You, and that is what I want for my children. Please help them to see that walking with You is tremendously worthwhile.

According to His Will

And this is the confidence that we have in him, that,
if we ask any thing according to his will, he heareth us.

1 JOHN 5:14

"Mommy, can I have candy? Mommy, can I have candy?" You get the idea, Lord. My son must have made his request a dozen times before I noticed. Clearly I did not wish to give him more candy. I know I've asked You for things in the past even when I knew they weren't good for me; but when I pray according to Your will, You hear and answer abundantly. Thank You!

Live by Faith

For therein is the righteousness of God revealed from
faith to faith: as it is written, The just shall live by faith.

ROMANS 1:17

I just received a letter from our missionary friends and shared bits of it with the children. My friends talked about the new building being erected for their church. As I read, my son asked, "Where do they get the money?" I explained that different churches helped them. "What if the churches don't?" he asked. Father, it was the perfect opportunity to explain that the just live by faith and that You provide for their needs.

By Grace through Faith

For by grace are ye saved through faith; and that not of yourselves: it is the gift of God: not of works, lest any man should boast.
EPHESIANS 2:8–9

I've found it surprising how many people think we are strange for not including Santa in our Christmas celebration. Our kids know that we love them and want to give them gifts regardless of how good or bad they've been. They trust there will be nice things under the tree. Your salvation is similar, Lord. You saved me because You love me. My salvation is by grace through faith, and no amount of good or bad behavior changes that.

God Will Fight Our Battles

With him is an arm of flesh; but with us is the LORD our God to help us, and to fight our battles.
2 CHRONICLES 32:8

Dear God, I want to raise my children by the instructions You have given, but at times it seems I'm in the front lines of a very heated battle. This world's standards are not based on Your Word, and they make it increasingly difficult to do right. You are on my side. My confidence is in You, and You will be victorious.

Wait for the Promise

*Behold, his soul which is lifted up is not upright
in him: but the just shall live by his faith.*

HABAKKUK 2:4

"When are we going to heaven?" my four-year-old asked. You know how hard it is for small children to grasp these things. I assured her You know the right time. "Well, I'm ready to go now so I won't have to eat my vegetables." It was humorous, God, but it was also an opportunity to teach her that You always keep Your promises. We don't always know how or when, but we trust that You will keep them.

Victory

*For whatsoever is born of God overcometh the world:
and this is the victory that overcometh the world, even our faith.*

1 JOHN 5:4

As my children act out their favorite Bible stories, they often ask for accessories to enhance their creativity. One thing I have to keep handy is a slingshot. David is my son's hero. Although the weapons fascinate him, the real attraction is the young boy who was able to defeat the mighty giant. Even at five he grasps what an extraordinary feat this was. He knows David won because of his faith in You.

A Reason to Believe

*Looking unto Jesus the author and finisher of our faith; who for
the joy that was set before him endured the cross, despising the
shame, and is set down at the right hand of the throne of God.*

HEBREWS 12:2

You are the best example of faith I could hope for, Lord Jesus. You knew all that You would face, and You went through with it anyway. All that You've ever done or will do gives me a reason to trust You. I can recall many times that I've been blessed when I've trusted in You, and I know that one day I'll receive the ultimate reward—eternity with You.

The Great Debate

*That your faith should not stand in the
wisdom of men, but in the power of God.*

1 Corinthians 2:5

My children are young, Father, and right now they believe most of what I tell them. They accept that You created us and the rest of the world. They have confidence in Your power. The day will come all too soon when their beliefs will be challenged by "the wisdom of men." Establish their faith in You now, Lord. Help them to understand that true wisdom comes from You.

Safety

*As for God, his way is perfect; the word of the LORD
is tried: he is a buckler to all them that trust in him.*

2 Samuel 22:31

As the mother of boys, I don't find it unusual to step on little green plastic army guys. Generally I'm too heavy, and they suffer a fatal blow. If they'd been in their jar where they belonged, they would have survived. It reminds me of the safety I have in You. The weight of the world can deliver crushing blows, but when my trust is in You where it belongs, I am safe.

Great Tasting

O taste and see that the LORD is good:
blessed is the man that trusteth in him.

PSALM 34:8

Father, I think some of my children's favorite preschool lessons centered on Psalm 34:8. They enjoyed assembling the lollipop-and-pipe-cleaner crafts and learning how the treats are made. Mostly I think they enjoyed sampling different kinds of candy. I pray though that the greatest lesson they learned is that a relationship with You is much sweeter than sugar, and the blessings of faith in You are much better than sweets.

With All Your Heart

Trust in the LORD with all thine heart;
and lean not unto thine own understanding.

PROVERBS 3:5

Lord, from the time my children were babies, I've committed them to Your care. When they were quite small, they looked to me for all the answers. As they grow, they realize that I don't know everything. I want them to understand, however, that You do and that everything is in Your control. Help them to commit daily to trusting You and to recognize that they don't have to face life alone.

Being Fruitful

Blessed is the man that trusteth in the LORD, and whose
hope the LORD is. For he shall be as a tree planted by the waters,
and that spreadeth out her roots by the river, and shall not see
when heat cometh, but her leaf shall be green; and shall not be
careful in the year of drought, neither shall cease from yielding fruit.

JEREMIAH 17:7–8

It's been a dry spring so far, Lord, and the garden is suffering
as a result. The kids have enjoyed filling their buckets with
water and distributing it among the plants. As the struggling
plants soak up the life-giving refreshment, I think about the
way that the lives of those who trust in You absorb the living
water and are fruitful beyond imagination.

Believe Only

But when Jesus heard it, he answered him, saying,
Fear not: believe only, and she shall be made whole.

LUKE 8:50

"Only believe." It sounds simple, Jesus, but this child was
dead! I know how concerned I was when my son lay ill in
his hospital bed—and his condition wasn't life-threatening.
I can't imagine how this man must have felt, but he obeyed.
He allowed You to return to his home, so he must have had
a certain amount of faith already. How greatly that faith
must have increased as he witnessed the miraculous resur-
rection of his daughter.

The Power of a Selfless Heart

Think back to the moment you first laid eyes on your beautiful child. Can you describe the love that engulfed your heart? Probably not. It's just one of those things too deep for words. Sometimes a feeling is best described through action rather than speech. You would do anything for that tiny helpless bundle in your arms.

As your child grows, so does your love, and it evolves in many different ways. Your desire is to meet her needs to the best of your ability. You enjoy spending time with her. You miss her when you are separated from her. You hurt when she cries. When discipline is necessary, it rips your heart out. You love her deeply, but you really can't explain the emotion.

There are many kinds of love. We say we love hot fudge sundaes, but that isn't what we mean. We might really enjoy hot fudge sundaes, but saying we love them is using the word too lightly. We say we love dogs, and that is possible. We care for them. We spend time with them, but our affection for them doesn't exceed our love for our families.

We love other people but probably not in the same way we love our own family. We might go out of our way to show others we care, but most of us would do more for our own children than we would for someone else's.

No matter what kind of love we have, it is limited. We are finite; compared to God, we are capable of offering only a small amount of love. Maybe that's why it is sometimes hard to comprehend the love of God. Romans 5:7–8 offers a glimpse into the depth of God's love: "For scarcely for a righteous man will one die: yet peradventure for a good man some would even dare to die. But God commendeth his love toward us, in that, while we were yet sinners, Christ died for us."

Charles Wesley captured the greatness of God's love in the hymn "And Can It Be?" He asks, "And can it be that I should gain an interest in my Savior's love?" We have an interest in—a portion of—God's love. All the love in our hearts doesn't come close to even that portion of love God has for me.

That should be a challenge to us. Our love can grow on a regular basis if we love through Christ. Take some time to read and meditate on the book of 1 John. Doing so will strengthen the love in your heart.

With All My Life

And thou shalt love the LORD thy God with all thine heart,
and with all thy soul, and with all thy might.

DEUTERONOMY 6:5

Jehovah God, You are the creator of all. Your power cannot be exceeded. You are above all, yet You want a personal love relationship with me. This truth is hard to comprehend, yet You require my total, undivided love. You want my entire devotion—my heart, soul, and strength. I cannot deny them. You, who have given me both physical and spiritual life, deserve only my best.

Follow Charity

Flee also youthful lusts: but follow righteousness,
faith, charity, peace, with them that call
on the Lord out of a pure heart.

2 TIMOTHY 2:22

During my teen years I faced a lot of pressure to fit in. It wasn't always easy to follow examples of righteousness, faith, love, and peace. It won't be long before my children are faced with similar situations. It's important we establish strong standards and convictions now, so that when temptation comes, they will choose love for You over lust of the flesh.

Misdirected Love

Love not the world, neither the things that are in the world.
If any man love the world, the love of the Father is not in him.

1 JOHN 2:15

Are my affections improper, dear Jesus? Am I too committed to the things of this world—my job, my children, my hobbies? Oh, I know these things have their proper place, but they should come after my love for You. Is it possible that I'm entertaining affection for things that should not be part of my life at all? Please make them clear to me and help me to eliminate them, for I want Your love in me.

A Love that Hurts

And she went, and sat her down over against him a good way off,
as it were a bow shot: for she said, Let me not see the death of the child.
And she sat over against him, and lift up her voice, and wept.
GENESIS 21:16

Oh God, how it must have hurt Hagar to know the son she cherished was suffering. He'd been cast from his father, and now he would die of thirst. It was more than she could bear. I too hate to see my children in pain. I love them, and it breaks my heart when they hurt. Help me to be strong for them and to bind their wounds when I can. Let us all remember that healing comes from You.

My First Love

Nevertheless I have somewhat against thee,
because thou hast left thy first love.
REVELATION 2:4

Forgive me, Lord Jesus. You have not been first place in my life as You should be. I've given too many excuses for why this might be so, but what it really comes down to is that my love has weakened. I've allowed too many things to come between us. I've been wrong, and I'm sorry. Let me be on fire for You once more. I want to return to You, my first love.

The Greatest Gift

For God so loved the world, that he gave his only begotten Son, that whosoever believeth in him should not perish, but have everlasting life.

JOHN 3:16

I think perhaps John 3:16 is the most famous passage in Your Word. I learned it as a child. My children have learned it, and I hope someday their kids will learn it also. For what good would the rest of Your Word be if it weren't for Your precious gift and amazing sacrifice? Although I cannot fully grasp Your love, I thank You for it.

Charity

Though I speak with the tongues of men and of angels, and have not charity, I am become as sounding brass, or a tinkling cymbal. . . . Charity suffereth long, and is kind; charity envieth not; charity vaunteth not itself, is not puffed up. . .beareth all things, believeth all things, hopeth all things, endureth all things. . . . And now abideth faith, hope, charity, these three; but the greatest of these is charity.

1 CORINTHIANS 13:1, 4, 7, 13

Getting the Right Order

He that loveth father or mother more than me is not worthy of me: and he that loveth son or daughter more than me is not worthy of me.

MATTHEW 10:37

Oh Lord, I love my husband and adore my children. It's hard to imagine anyone or anything to whom I'd rather devote my time, but I need to make sure my priorities are straight. Help me to ensure that the time I give them doesn't take away from what I give You. Oh, give me a desire to make You first.

Serving God in Love

But take diligent heed to do the commandment and the law, which Moses the servant of the LORD charged you, to love the LORD your God, and to walk in all his ways, and to keep his commandments, and to cleave unto him, and to serve him with all your heart and with all your soul.

JOSHUA 22:5

Lord, I understand true love involves service; that is the object of love. At times though, my kids make overwhelming demands, and I become frustrated that I can't even sit down to a meal without their requesting something. I have to recognize that love involves service and sacrifice. It's true of my love for You too. I must serve You 100 percent always.

Abounding Love

And this I pray, that your love may abound yet more and more in knowledge and in all judgment.

PHILIPPIANS 1:9

I don't think anything is more powerful than love. When I enter my baby's room in the morning and I see her angelic smile and chubby arms reaching toward me, I feel her love, and my heart overflows. Yet I know the love we share is incomplete without You. You are the author of this great blessing, and the closer we become to You, the more our love will abound. What joy that is!

Love and Correction

For whom the LORD loveth he correcteth;
even as a father the son in whom he delighteth.
PROVERBS 3:12

Master Artist, You know how creative my daughter is. I'm thankful You designed her that way. She has added beautiful splashes of color to my world. It's just that I didn't want red crayon streaks across my counters. I didn't like making her scrub the marks off, and she liked it even less, but I needed to teach her there are proper times and places for artwork. Lord, when I must discipline, let it be with love.

Cheap Talk

My little children, let us not love in word,
neither in tongue; but in deed and in truth.
1 JOHN 3:18

Father, there is no greater example of the saying "Actions speak louder than words" than where love is concerned. Oh God, how I love my precious children, but I shouldn't have to try to convince anyone—especially them—of this truth. It should just be obvious in the way I treat them. Unfortunately, my tone of voice or lack of attention often conveys other messages. Forgive me, Lord. Give me the patience to show my kids I love them.

Rebekah Loved Jacob

And Isaac loved Esau, because he did eat
of his venison: but Rebekah loved Jacob.
GENESIS 25:28

Father, I'm tempted to look at the faults of Isaac and Rebekah and to say they shouldn't have been playing favorites, but what I also notice is Rebekah loved Jacob simply because he was her son. While I don't wish to show partiality among my children, I do pray for the ability to love them unconditionally, because each is a precious miracle from You.

The Power of Love

Hatred stirreth up strifes: but love covereth all sins.
PROVERBS 10:12

I know we live in a fallen world, Lord. Evil abounds, and hatred and prejudice come easily. But these are bitter attitudes that poison the soul. Loving the unlovely is much more difficult, but when love permeates my soul, it opens my eyes and helps me realize that the other person needs You. God, please help me to love all people and to teach my children to do the same.

The Power of Connection

Kristen was unpacking again. She sighed as she opened a box of her children's toys. She was glad that her husband, Joe, had been called into the ministry, but she wondered if they would ever truly find a place to call home. Joe had always felt that God wanted him to be a pastor, but for the first several years after they'd been married, he had worked in associate or youth positions, as well as in other areas of the church. Now he'd accepted the pastorate in a small rural community.

Would this be the place they would settle down and call home? In some ways Kristen hoped so. It seemed like a safe, quiet place to raise their children. On the other hand, it was almost too quiet for her. She was used to being surrounded by family and friends. How would she get to know anyone here?

As she looked out her kitchen window, she saw two unfamiliar children approaching her own. About that time there was a knock at her door. She answered to find a young woman smiling at her.

"Hi, I'm April," the woman said. "I live next door, and I've brought a meat loaf for your supper. I hope you don't mind that my kids stayed in the yard with yours. They couldn't wait to meet them."

At first Kristen was overwhelmed by the woman's bubbling personality, but her cheerful smile was infectious. Soon the two women were laughing like old friends. As their meeting came to an end, Kristen confessed, "I'm glad to be part of Joe's ministry, but I was a little afraid to move to such a 'country' place. I was afraid I'd be bored and unable to make friends."

"I felt the same way when we moved here five years ago," April said. "I quickly realized that although it's different from what I was used to, it's never dull. Plus I've made some of my most precious friendships since living here."

Kristen was grateful for the friendship that April initiated that day. They formed a lifelong bond, and later Kristen found herself reaching out to other newcomers and forging more friendships.

God established friends and family for many purposes. These special people stick with us during good times and bad. Spending time with those we love is a tremendous encouragement, for there really is strength in numbers (Ecclesiastes 4:9–12). We need friends, and God will provide them. We must be careful whom we choose for our closest friends though, because they need to be individuals who will encourage us to glorify God.

Be sure to thank God today for your friends and family.

The Right Friends

My son, if sinners entice thee, consent thou not.
PROVERBS 1:10

Oh Lord, it's hard for children to find good friends. They experience so much negative peer pressure and so much exposure to temptation. Please protect my children. Give me the wisdom to guide them in choosing friends who please You. Please provide opportunities for them to meet other godly young people, and help them to be good examples. Give them a desire to do what's right and to run from temptation.

Saving the Family

And the young men that were spies went in, and brought out Rahab, and her father, and her mother, and her brethren, and all that she had; and they brought out all her kindred, and left them without the camp of Israel.
JOSHUA 6:23

Perhaps Rahab didn't have the best reputation in Jericho, but she obviously loved her family. When she had the opportunity to save them, she didn't hesitate. Whoever was with her was spared destruction.

Several other Bible passages reflect people's concern for their families as well, such as the account of Noah and the flood, or the account of the Israelites and the first Passover in Egypt. Now You want me to show the same concern. I will invite my family into the security of Your love.

The Name of God

*I will declare thy name unto my brethren:
in the midst of the congregation will I praise thee.*

PSALM 22:22

Many of my relatives and acquaintances don't know You, Lord. They've never experienced Your amazing love. It is my duty to declare Your name among them. Too often I am so focused on the needs of my own children that I tune out all other needs, but I must share Your love with my friends and family. They should know how great You are.

Together

*Two are better than one; because they
have a good reward for their labour.*

ECCLESIASTES 4:9

It's sad to see people cutting themselves off from others. My children are only beginning to understand the concept of friendship. Although my daughter will play with or interact with a number of children, she's convinced that she can have only one friend. Unfortunately, this notion sometimes shows up in her behavior. Please give me patience as I work with her. Help her to be a friend to those around her.

Clearing the Record

I've been holding a grudge against a fellow believer. I have called her names and labeled her unkindly. I will face the consequences. I have brought a gift to You, Lord, and I want You to bless it. First I must go to my friend and straighten things out between us. I will leave my gift and humbly beg my friend's forgiveness. Then I will make my offering to You (Based on Matthew 5:22–24).

Brotherly Love

Be kindly affectioned one to another with brotherly love;
in honour preferring one another.
ROMANS 12:10

I know You've blessed me with brothers, Lord, and I thank You for them. Ours is more than a casual love. It is a blood bond that keeps us together through thick and thin. It's the kind of tie I should have with my Christian brothers and sisters too, for the blood that binds us together is even stronger than my earthly bond with my brothers. Oh, how I rejoice in the sense of belonging You've given me!

A Trustworthy Friend

For I have no man likeminded,
who will naturally care for your state.
PHILIPPIANS 2:20

I want my children to understand the importance of being friendly to their peers. However, I ask that they would use discretion in choosing their closest companions. Help them to select friends who love You. Lead my kids to those who are trustworthy, dependable, and responsible. Let their friends be those who would encourage them spiritually. Most of all, help each of my children to be that kind of friend.

In-Laws

*It hath fully been shewed me, all that thou hast done unto thy
mother in law since the death of thine husband: and how thou
hast left thy father and thy mother, and the land of thy nativity,
and art come unto a people which thou knewest not heretofore.*

RUTH 2:11

The challenges of combining two people with unique back-grounds often bring on the in-law jokes. Ruth's story, how-ever, is amazing. She had a heritage far different from her husband's, yet when he died she left her own country and family to care for Naomi. What love they shared. Lord, let me be that kind of daughter-in-law, and when it's my turn, let me be a good mother-in-law.

My Best Friend

*A man that hath friends must shew himself friendly:
and there is a friend that sticketh closer than a brother.*

PROVERBS 18:24

Thank You, dear Jesus, for being my best friend. There have been times when I've been disappointed by friends or family, but You will never let me down. I know my children might have friends who will hurt them. Help them realize that You are the best friend they will ever have. You will be with them during their brightest and darkest moments. You will never desert them.

Christ First

*And another of his disciples said unto him, Lord,
suffer me first to go and bury my father. But Jesus said
unto him, Follow me; and let the dead bury their dead.*

MATTHEW 8:21–22

I know it seems to many that You were being selfish when You told Your follower he couldn't bury his father, but he was saying he didn't want to follow You completely until his father (who could have been quite healthy) had died. There's nothing wrong with being dedicated to our families, but our devotion to You must be first. It's not always easy, but Your way is always right.

No Strife

And Abram said unto Lot, Let there be no strife, I pray thee, between me and thee, and between my herdmen and thy herdmen; for we be brethren.
GENESIS 13:8

As I look around, I am saddened by the number of families who can't get along. Often it seems they can't even remember what the original problem was. Father, protect my family from such a breach. I know we won't always agree on everything, but help us to work out our differences humbly and lovingly. We are family. You put us together for a reason. Don't let there be strife among us.

Good Wounds and Bad Kisses

Faithful are the wounds of a friend;
but the kisses of an enemy are deceitful.
PROVERBS 27:6

Flattery is so destructive, God. Many people are just waiting to smooth-talk my children and lead them astray. Please give them friends who are willing to offer constructive criticism if the need arises. Although it might be humbling, let them realize the wounds only hurt for a while and will make them more mature people. The enemy's poisonous kiss, however, can bring long-term trouble.

Friends and Siblings

A friend loveth at all times,
and a brother is born for adversity.
PROVERBS 17:17

What a privilege it has been to watch my children become best friends with each other. Of course they have the typical sibling fights, but they are also very protective of each other. They really enjoy spending time together. I pray that through the years they'll continue to be there for one another. I ask You to help them encourage each other in their walks with You. Help them realize what blessings they have in siblings who are also friends.

The Three-Legged Race

Can two walk together, except they be agreed?
AMOS 3:3

I laughed as my children participated in a three-legged race. Despite the significant difference in their height, they'd insisted on being partners. They had a blast, but without winning results. The incident reminded me that while choosing ungodly friends might seem fun for a while, it can have disastrous results. Help me to choose friends who please You, and as my kids are forming friendships in their early years, help them to remember their three-legged race.

The Power of Belonging

Over the years Stacey attended many Fourth of July celebrations, and she never grew tired of them. It wasn't until recently, however, that she was moved to tears by the fireworks display. She was sitting in a grassy area with her family surrounded by hundreds of other people. Everyone was oohing and aahing, as is often the case. Children were laughing and adding their comments at each burst of color.

All at once "Taps" began to play over the loudspeaker. The crowd became silent as everyone respectfully stood to their feet. All of the fireworks were red, white, and blue. When "Taps" ended, "Proud to Be an American" began. The crowd remained standing until the song ended. Then the applause was deafening. Many tears were brushed away as people considered the blood that had been shed and the sacrifices that had been made so that they could enjoy so much. With the exception of her own family, Stacey didn't know anyone around her, but at that moment she felt a strong connection with her fellow Americans. They were part of something big—something special.

Stacey felt very proud to be an American. She thought about the freedoms and opportunities here and the way God truly had blessed her. She was saddened to realize though that even Christians have deserted Him.

We've become so proud of our own accomplishments that we have unwittingly shut God out of our lives. As a result, He has become increasingly excluded from our homes, our schools, and our government. We have seen the negative consequences of this in many ways, and at times we've given up hope. But it's not too late. God can still bless this great nation if we let Him (Psalm 33:12).

What we need is for a revival to sweep across our country. It could happen, but it must begin in our own hearts. When God does a work in individual lives, those lives work together, and revival affects their communities and eventually their nation (Zechariah 8:20–23).

Begin today by thanking God for your nation. Seek His forgiveness on behalf of the land. Pray for revival and healing. Pray for your children, and teach them what it means to belong to a wonderful country. Be a part of inviting God back in.

A Nation under God

*Blessed is the nation whose God is the LORD; and the
people whom he hath chosen for his own inheritance.*

PSALM 33:12

Thank You, God, for this great nation. You've blessed us
in countless ways. In the beginning our hearts were turned
toward You, but we have strayed far from You. I fear for my
children and grandchildren. I want them to experience what
it's like to be part of a God-honoring people. Oh, give us
revival. Turn us back to You.

A Better Country

*But now they desire a better country, that is, an heavenly:
wherefore God is not ashamed to be called their God:
for he hath prepared for them a city.*

HEBREWS 11:16

I'm thrilled that my kids love their country. As patriotic songs
play, they become excited, and they can spot the star-spangled
banner a mile away. Just the other day my daughter even
included an American flag in her sidewalk chalk drawing.
But Lord, even at their young ages, they are already begging
to go to heaven. They are proud little Americans, but they
know something better is waiting for them.

All Nations Shall Worship Thee

*Among the gods there is none like unto thee, O Lord; neither are
there any works like unto thy works. All nations whom thou hast
made shall come and worship before thee, O Lord; and shall glorify
thy name. For thou art great, and doest wondrous things: thou art
God alone. Teach me thy way, O LORD; I will walk in thy truth:
unite my heart to fear thy name. I will praise thee, O Lord my God,
with all my heart: and I will glorify thy name for evermore.*

PSALM 86:8–12

God Is in Control

When he giveth quietness, who then can make trouble?
and when he hideth his face, who then can behold him?
whether it be done against a nation, or against a man only.

JOB 34:29

I'm glad You're in charge, God. We hear of many countries that want to destroy us. They can do nothing unless You allow it though. I'm grateful that You are in control and that nothing takes You by surprise. Sometimes I'm tempted to worry—to take my family and run—but no matter where I am, I know that You make no mistakes.

Exaltation or Reproach

Righteousness exalteth a nation:
but sin is a reproach to any people.

PROVERBS 14:34

I have tried to teach my children the importance of living for You. I want them to understand that obedience is good for them and for their country. Lord, if only more people would realize that each individual's righteousness contributes to that of the whole nation. So many of us want Your blessing, but we refuse to live for You. Then we wonder why we face reproach. Forgive us, Father, and make us righteous.

Thank You for Our Leaders

I exhort therefore that, first of all, supplications, prayers,
intercessions, and giving of thanks, be made for all men;
for kings, and for all that are in authority; that we may
lead a quiet and peaceable life in all godliness and honesty.

1 TIMOTHY 2:1–2

Managing this nation is not a job I would want—managing my household involves enough challenges! I'm thankful for those who are willing to dedicate their time and effort to govern the people of this land. I don't always agree with them, but I can let them know that. I ask that You would help these men and women make wise choices. Help them also to remember that this nation was founded on biblical principles.

The Lord Will Be Avenged

Shall I not visit for these things? saith the LORD:
shall not my soul be avenged on such a nation as this?
A wonderful and horrible thing is committed in the land.
JEREMIAH 5:29–30

As much as I love America, I have to admit it sometimes terrifies me. When I was growing up, I felt reasonably safe. My parents were allowed to raise me according to biblical standards. Although I still have that privilege, the drift toward a humanistic viewpoint is happening at an alarming speed. You won't tolerate this much longer. You will be avenged for the wrong we've committed. Oh God, send revival before it's too late.

God Gives the Power

By me kings reign, and princes decree justice.
PROVERBS 8:15

It seems that being entrusted with responsibility brings pride. Even my toddler wants to help put away spoons or forks. So it goes without saying that most individuals who lead a country are glad to be in that position. Father, remind them often that You gave them the responsibility and that they must conduct their duties in a way that pleases You.

An Unusual Source

*Notwithstanding, lest we should offend them, go thou to the sea,
and cast an hook, and take up the fish that first cometh up;
and when thou hast opened his mouth, thou shalt find a piece
of money: that take, and give unto them for me and thee.*

MATTHEW 17:27

It's not that I don't want to do my part to pay taxes. The
problem is wondering where the money will come from. My
kids think I can just go to the bank or pull cash from my
purse anytime they want something. Sometimes I think the
government feels that way too. It's not that simple though.
Even so, You got Your tax money from a fish, and I know You
can provide for me.

God-Ordained Power

*Let every soul be subject unto the higher powers. For there is
no power but of God: the powers that be are ordained of God.*

ROMANS 13:1

"What's good for me is good for me; what's good for you
is fine for you"—this attitude seems to be a growing trend.
It's a "do your own thing" world. No one wants to answer to
anyone else. You've given us higher authorities for a reason
though. Without parents, teachers, bosses, and government,
and especially without You, chaos would reign. We might not
always like established rules, but we still need to obey them.

The Kingdom Is the Lord's

For the kingdom is the LORD's:
and he is the governor among the nations.

PSALM 22:28

I know our government is supposedly "by the people, for the people." That sounds nice, but really it should be "by God, for God," shouldn't it, Lord? That's the only way it can really be for the people. It's like anything else. When You're in first place, everything else will fall into place. I pray more people will understand this truth so that as a nation we will let You be in control.

Elections

The king's heart is in the hand of the LORD,
as the rivers of water: he turneth it whithersoever he will.

PROVERBS 21:1

I truly am grateful for the privilege to vote, God, but sometimes it makes me uneasy. With the growing lack of regard for You that has infiltrated our nation, I'm concerned about who will be chosen to lead our country and how the election results will affect the future of my kids. I know You are in control of who is chosen and how they will govern. Although the situation might look bleak, everything is in Your hands. Lord, help me to trust You.

Paying for Crime

*And whosoever will not do the law of thy God, and the law of the king,
let judgment be executed speedily upon him, whether it be unto death,
or to banishment, or to confiscation of goods, or to imprisonment.*

EZRA 7:26

Children are not particularly fond of the discipline that
follows wrongdoing. I discipline my children to help them
understand that their actions affect other people. As they
grow, they must follow the laws of the community and nation,
or the consequences will be much greater than what they face
now. Lord, please make them good citizens.

God's Choice

*Thou shalt in any wise set him king over thee,
whom the LORD thy God shall choose.*

DEUTERONOMY 17:15

As I consider the nations, I wonder how evil people came
to be the leaders of certain countries. I have to believe it's
because somewhere along the line, people failed to obey
You and let You choose their leader. Please help me not to
be guilty of disobedience. May I always seek Your guidance
when it's time to vote. Please give us strong leaders who will
obey You.

My Praise

The Power of an Overflowing Heart

We are blessed to live in a geographically diverse land. From the coastlines to the mountains to the open plain, we can observe the majesty of our Creator. If you live where few lights adulterate the night sky, you should make it a point to go outside on a clear night and watch the stars. Consider all that is actually contained in those pinpoints of brightness.

God's greatness truly is beyond our comprehension. Maybe that's why so many people reject Him. They can't understand Him, and it's easier to believe all of creation got here by chance. When we're honest with ourselves, we must admit this universe had to have a wise and intelligent creator. This truth is hard to fathom, but what is even harder to grasp is that He made each of us unique, and He takes a special interest in each individual. Is it any wonder David said, "The heavens declare the glory of God; and the firmament sheweth his handywork" (Psalm 19:1)?

In Psalm 150, a beautiful psalm of praise, we are challenged, "Let every thing that hath breath praise the LORD. Praise ye the LORD" (v. 6). Have you taken this command seriously? I think often we get so caught up in the busyness of our days that our talks with God are a brief thanks for the day and a list of what we want or need. We really don't think about the One we are addressing. We forget that we are bowing before the almighty, all-wise

God of the universe. We should be offering a sacrifice of sincere praise and worship.

Maybe this seems somewhat awkward to you if you are not used to including praise in your prayers. Start by singing hymns of adoration. God won't mind if you're a bit off key—He made your voice exactly the way He wanted to. He's more interested in the attitude behind the song. You also might consider keeping a praise journal. Fill it with all the wonderful things you know and learn about your Savior. Begin talking to God about what you write. Soon your worship will become more natural, and you won't be able to keep from praising God.

Creation Will Praise God

*Sing, O heavens; and be joyful, O earth; and break forth
into singing, O mountains: for the LORD hath comforted
his people, and will have mercy upon his afflicted.*

ISAIAH 49:13

I was made to praise You and Your great majesty, oh God. In fact, all creation—the heavens, the earth, the mountains—all Your works declare Your glory. Yet even in Your greatness You take time to offer comfort to Your people. Even with our imperfections You have mercy on us. You truly are a great God, worthy of infinitely more honor than I am capable of bestowing upon You.

A Chosen Generation

*But ye are a chosen generation, a royal priesthood, an holy nation,
a peculiar people; that ye should shew forth the praises of him who
hath called you out of darkness into his marvellous light.*

1 PETER 2:9

Each new generation has so much to offer, Lord. I'll never forget the moment my firstborn entered the world and my husband leaned over and whispered, "It's a boy." How much hope we felt. There was so much we wanted for our tiny son, but our greatest desire was that he would one day become part of Your chosen generation—that he would sing Your praises. Lord, the day of his second birth was even more spectacular than that of his first!

Even at Midnight

*And at midnight Paul and Silas prayed, and sang
praises unto God: and the prisoners heard them.*

Acts 16:25

For the past two weeks, the baby has not slept well. She seems
to need that extra bit of comfort. Last night as I was rocking
her and quietly singing hymns, she snuggled in and relaxed. It
struck me that when we sing praises to You, our worship is a
blessing to others. Although I'm ready for a full night's sleep,
I can now look at those midnight meetings with a different
attitude.

In Him Is Victory

*I will call on the LORD, who is worthy to be praised:
so shall I be saved from mine enemies.*

2 Samuel 22:4

Lord, You are worthy of all my adoration. I'm amazed at how
much I am blessed when I praise You. When I'm glorifying
You, I feel Your strength. I know You are with me in a special
way. I want my entire existence to be centered on You, for
You are awesome. Without You my life would lie in shattered
ruins, but You give me victory.

Thou Art Exalted

*Thine, O LORD is the greatness, and the power, and the glory,
and the victory, and the majesty: for all that is in the heaven and
in the earth is thine; thine is the kingdom, O LORD, and thou
art exalted as head above all. Both riches and honour come of thee,
and thou reignest over all; and in thine hand is power and might;
and in thine hand it is to make great, and to give strength unto all.
Now therefore, our God, we thank thee, and praise thy glorious name.*

1 Chronicles 29:11–13

The Heavenly Choir

*And they sing the song of Moses the servant of God, and the
song of the Lamb, saying, Great and marvellous are thy works,
Lord God Almighty; just and true are thy ways, thou King of saints.*
REVELATION 15:3

We sat amazed as the young people in our church sang,
"Great and marvelous are Thy works, Lord God Almighty."
They sang with deep joy and sincerity. I began to think about
how that same song will be even more beautiful when we
hear it in the perfection of heaven. Lord, how truly wonderful
You are!

Meaningful Routine

*And to stand every morning to thank and
praise the LORD, and likewise at even.*
1 CHRONICLES 23:30

All the books on child-rearing say how important it is to
establish routines for children. It makes sense. I generally do
better with a schedule too. You must have known we would
need order, because You've told us what to include in our
daily routine. Each morning we need to begin by praising
You. We're also to end the day by praising You. Doing so
helps us to recall Your blessings and greatness. Praising You
gives us the right perspective.

With My Whole Heart

I will praise thee, O LORD, with my whole heart; I will shew forth all thy marvellous works. I will be glad and rejoice in thee: I will sing praise to thy name, O thou most High. When mine enemies are turned back, they shall fall and perish at thy presence. For thou hast maintained my right and my cause; thou satest in the throne judging right.

PSALM 9:1–4

The Stones Would Cry Out

And he answered and said unto them, I tell you that, if these should hold their peace, the stones would immediately cry out.

LUKE 19:40

Sometimes it feels like our children are forbidden to praise You at school, dear God. In many instances adults aren't allowed to mention You in the workplace either. I would love to be there when the stones begin to sing Your praises. I would love to witness the reactions of those who made these wicked rules. Even better though would be the joy of seeing those who once rejected You come to know You and begin to join in the chorus glorifying You.

All Ye People

And again, praise the Lord, all ye Gentiles; and laud him, all ye people.

ROMANS 15:11

Thank You, Lord, that all people are important to You. Thank You that even I am instructed to praise You. You've done so much for me every day of my life. You give me strength and breath. You meet all my needs abundantly. You've blessed me with a beautiful family. The list goes on and on and is topped by the gift of Your precious Son. I cannot help but praise You.

The Marriage of the Lamb

And I saw an angel standing in the sun; and he cried with a loud voice,
saying to all the fowls that fly in the midst of heaven, Come and
gather yourselves together unto the supper of the great God.
REVELATION 19:17

I've attended or participated in more weddings than I can count. Mostly they've been happy occasions, but my own was my favorite. Even that can't compare to the rejoicing that will take place the day You and Your bride are joined. I look forward to rejoicing with so many others the day that celebration takes place. I only ask that my children and loved ones will be there to join in on that glorious day.

All My Days

While I live will I praise the LORD: I will sing
praises unto my God while I have any being.
PSALM 146:2

Each day You give me is a gift from You. I cannot help but praise You. Each breath is a blessing that must be taken in Your honor. The life I live should be a testament to Your greatness. My children, neighbors, and everyone I meet should be able to tell I've been walking with You. Lord, while I live and breathe, I will praise You.

Thou Art Lord Alone

Stand up and bless the LORD your God for ever and ever:
and blessed be thy glorious name, which is exalted above all blessing
and praise. Thou, even thou, art LORD alone; thou hast made
heaven, the heaven of heavens, with all their host, the earth, and all
things that are therein, the seas, and all that is therein, and thou
preservest them all; and the host of heaven worshippeth thee.
NEHEMIAH 9:5–6

Walking with God

*The fear of the LORD is the beginning of wisdom: a good understanding
have all they that do his commandments: his praise endureth for ever.*
<small>PSALM 111:10</small>

Father, I've tried to teach my children that there is good fear
and bad fear. Please help them to understand that fearing
You is the first step in walking with You. As their respect for
You grows, they will want to know more about You and will
choose to obey You. As they obey You, they will get to know
You and adore You more fully. They will begin to praise You
fervently.

The Power of Completion

Have you just tucked your children into bed? Maybe you are up waiting for one of your teens to come home from a late job or an evening out with friends. Perhaps your grown children have left home, but as your day winds down, you find yourself thinking about and praying for them. How has motherhood fulfilled you? As Christians we believe the opportunity to positively influence our offspring for the cause of Christ is a high calling and one that brings great blessing. What a joy to watch our children come to Christ and begin to serve Him and to know we played a part in that decision. Motherhood, with all its ups and downs, truly is fulfilling.

There are other ways a Christian mother can find fulfillment though. How many passages of scripture challenge us to do everything to God's glory? (Colossians 3:17 is one example of many.) When we go about our tasks in a way that honors God, we are sure to find His fulfillment. It might seem ridiculous to think that paying bills on time or sweeping the front porch would be chores God would notice, but He does care. He knows the attitude with which we approach our tasks, and He blesses us accordingly. Yes, we really can find fulfillment in our day-to-day responsibilities.

What kind of wife are you? Being a good and godly wife brings fulfillment similar to that which results from being a good and godly mother. Do you pray regularly for your husband? Do you encourage him? Are you a helpmeet for him? The world often portrays the wife as a bossy, whiny nag. The Bible gives a far different picture, and when we follow the Bible's instruction, we find far greater fulfillment.

Each of us has an occupation, whether it be at home or at a place of employment. I'm sure there are times we've all agreed with the old saying "The grass is greener on the other side." It might seem true but only when we lose sight of God. Even if you don't care for your job, try to keep Philippians 4:11 in mind. Do your best in every situation, and pray God will show you what He has to fulfill you. When we are doing His will, we will be the most fulfilled.

Righteous Children

The father of the righteous shall greatly rejoice: and he that begetteth a wise child shall have joy of him. Thy father and thy mother shall be glad.
PROVERBS 23:24–25

Dear God, from the moment my first child was conceived, my greatest calling has been to bring up my children in the nurture and admonition of You. As each of my children calls on You for salvation, part of my life's work is fulfilled. I am hoping to hear, "Well done," one day, and I also anticipate standing with my children as they hear those words.

Why Am I Here?

And who knoweth whether thou art come to the kingdom for such a time as this?
ESTHER 4:14

Father, I can think of a few women in the Bible who knew what You had planned for their children, but that's not usually the case. I think of Nancy Lincoln and of D. L. Moody's mother. They probably had no idea how their sons would affect this nation. I don't know what You have planned for my children either, but You have chosen me to be their mother and to prepare them to help make a difference—small or great.

What Is Success?

Because thou hast forgotten the God of thy salvation. . .in the day shalt thou make thy plant to grow, and in the morning shalt thou make thy seed to flourish: but the harvest shall be a heap in the day of grief and of desperate sorrow.
ISAIAH 17:10–11

Lord, please help me to remember that true success lies in pleasing You. It's not that I don't want my family to dress well or have nice things. I enjoy being able to go to fun places with my husband and children, but help me never to sacrifice my relationship with You to do these things. I would rather please You than be a worldly success.

All That God Commands

And they answered Joshua, saying, All that thou commandest us we will do, and whithersoever thou sendest us, we will go.
JOSHUA 1:16

The people of Israel recognized that Joshua was giving them Your message and that it was You they were obeying. You've given me Your Word and the Holy Spirit to direct me, Lord. Although I don't always understand Your command, I want to obey. I know that the greatest satisfaction comes from doing Your will. Sometimes I'm not sure how I will accomplish these things, but You always make a way, and joy is the result.

Seek Ye First

But seek ye first the kingdom of God, and his righteousness; and all these things shall be added unto you.
MATTHEW 6:33

One of my favorite scripture choruses comes from Matthew 6:33. It stirs up memories of school days when my classmates and I would be especially fired up about putting You first. We're all adults now, many of us with children of our own, and I have to wonder how many of us want this chorus to be a favorite among our children. Lord, rekindle the revival fire in my heart. I want to pass it on to my kids.

The Official "Garden Hoer"

Sow to yourselves in righteousness, reap in mercy;
break up your fallow ground: for it is time to seek the
LORD, till he come and rain righteousness upon you.

HOSEA 10:12

There was an empty spot in our garden—well, empty of anything but weeds. I wanted to plant sweet corn, but the ground needed some attention. My son dubbed himself my official "garden hoer." Soon the ground was ready. The seed was planted, the rains came, and the corn began to grow.

Lord, work up the ground in my heart. Sow seeds of righteousness. Make the planting and growing conditions good, and let me be productive for You.

Fires and Paper Plates

Every man's work shall be made manifest: for the day
shall declare it, because it shall be revealed by fire;
and the fire shall try every man's work of what sort it is.

1 CORINTHIANS 3:13

We had a hot dog roast recently, and my children discovered the thrill of tossing the plates into the fire and watching them disappear. I've done it too, Lord, but this time I thought about how that plate was just temporarily useful. Once it met the flame, it was gone.

Father, show me the things in my life that are worthless. Help me get rid of them before I am consumed by worldliness. Help me focus on things that will last.

My Vocation

I therefore, the prisoner of the Lord, beseech you that ye
walk worthy of the vocation wherewith ye are called.

EPHESIANS 4:1

I've tried many career paths, Father, and I have enjoyed most of them, but not one compares to being a mother. It seems the more I invest in my children, the more I am rewarded. It's especially true spiritually speaking, and I know that walking with You and teaching my kids to do the same is my highest calling. Lord, help us all to walk worthily of the calling You've given us.

A Great Compliment

Then Paul answered, What mean ye to weep and to break mine heart? for I am ready not to be bound only, but also to die at Jerusalem for the name of the Lord Jesus.

ACTS 21:13

I don't think Paul really had a death wish, although he was looking forward to being with Jesus. It's just that he recognized that to die because of his testimony would be a compliment of the highest kind. I've thought about that, and I've wondered what would happen to my kids if I were gone. I know You'd take care of them. So Lord, let me live completely for You, no matter what the cost.

Finishing the Job

As the LORD commanded Moses his servant, so did Moses command Joshua, and so did Joshua; he left nothing undone of all that the LORD commanded Moses.

JOSHUA 11:15

It's hard for children to grasp the concept of completing a task well. If the toys are off the floor, the cleanup is suitable (even if they're in a pile on the bed). They don't understand how rewarding it is to finish the job. I know I must set the example with each job You give me. Each day that You help me complete my work, I feel useful and fulfilled.

Christ in Me

I am crucified with Christ: nevertheless I live; yet not I, but Christ liveth in me: and the life which I now live in the flesh I live by the faith of the Son of God, who loved me, and gave himself for me.

GALATIANS 2:20

Recently I was sharing Your love with a young mother. She has been through some trials lately, and she seemed fascinated by what I said. But Lord, she has some things she just doesn't want to give up. I told her if she accepted You, You'd replace those negative things and help her to become a new person. She's close, Lord, but she's just not sure. Open her heart and help her see how fulfilling life will be with You.

Searching for God

And ye shall seek me, and find me, when ye shall search for me with all your heart.

JEREMIAH 29:13

I searched frantically for my son this morning. He'd been playing in the yard, and when I went to do a load of laundry, he disappeared. I hadn't heard him come in, but I checked his room anyway. I was relieved to find him there asleep.

I know You don't disappear, God, but at times I lose sight of You. With longing I search for You, and when I find You, I feel complete once more.

Working on Perfect

Not as though I had already attained, either were already
perfect: but I follow after, if that I may apprehend that
for which also I am apprehended of Christ Jesus.
PHILIPPIANS 3:12

I know You're still working on me, God. My ultimate goal is
Christ-likeness. I know I won't totally achieve it while I'm
on earth, but I will do my best. With Your help, I will come
closer to the goal. I'll make mistakes, but I won't give up.
I'll keep trying until the day I stand before You. Then I'll be
like You, for I'll see You as You are.

A Crown of Righteousness

Lord, when my earthly life is ending, I want to be able
to say, "For I am now ready to be offered, and the time of
my departure is at hand. I have fought a good fight, I have
finished my course, I have kept the faith: henceforth there
is laid up for me a crown of righteousness, which the Lord,
the righteous judge, shall give me at that day: and not to
me only, but unto all them also that love his appearing"
(2 Timothy 4:6–8).

My History

The Power of Experience

Do you remember your parents ever saying something like, "Believe me; I know. I've been there"? Chances are you didn't want to pay attention to their words at the time, but you're probably seeing things in a different light now that you're a mother. You've probably realized by now just how beneficial your past—good or bad—can be as long as you have learned from it.

Our history can work to benefit our children's training. How often have you heard one of your children ask, "Mommy, when you were a little girl. . . ?" Perhaps the questioning stems from mere curiosity, but so often it presents a wonderful, teachable moment. When we look at the past, we can easily see the results of actions. To a child, the concrete reality of what occurred is much more substantial than possible consequences of a future action.

Our past is important, whether we are proud of it or embarrassed by it. If we are happy with our history, we must acknowledge God's grace in the situation. Sometimes people with a "clean slate" don't want to share their testimonies because they feel they aren't exciting enough and no one will listen. It's simply not true. Think about all of the basically good people in the world who are still unsaved and on their way to hell. It just might take another basically good, but saved by grace, person to show them the truth about their spiritual condition. Be glad your history is clean, and let God use you abundantly.

On the other hand, you might have a past you are ashamed of. Don't lose hope. Think of the many biblical examples of leaders with shameful, negative histories. The apostle Paul is one of the most prominent, and he willingly exposed his past to help lead others to Christ. Or consider Rahab, Ruth, Matthew, Zacchaeus, the woman at the well—the list goes on. These people didn't wallow in the past. They gave their lives to God and became shining examples for Him.

Many of us fall somewhere in the middle between "good" and "bad." We've done our best, but we've made mistakes. That's how it was with David—the man after God's own heart. Like him, we should seek forgiveness from God and from ourselves. We must learn from our errors and go on living for God. Decide today to let your history be your friend rather than your enemy.

My God from Birth

For thou art my hope, O Lord GOD: thou art my trust from my youth.
By thee have I been holden up from the womb: thou art he that took
me out of my mother's bowels: my praise shall be continually of thee.
I am as a wonder unto many; but thou art my strong refuge. Let my
mouth be filled with thy praise and with thy honour all the day.

PSALM 71:5–8

Growing Up

When I was a child, I spake as a child, I understood
as a child, I thought as a child: but when I became
a man, I put away childish things.

1 CORINTHIANS 13:11

When my children first started talking, I loved to hear their babyish chatter. It was precious and beautiful, but as their speech advanced, I was happy for their complex sentences and proud of their expanding vocabulary. I know You want me to grow too, Lord. The baby steps were fine after the early days of my salvation, but You want me to move from the past to being more like You, and with Your help I will.

Moving beyond the Past

Therefore remove sorrow from thy heart, and put away
evil from thy flesh: for childhood and youth are vanity.

ECCLESIASTES 11:10

There are times, Father, when I am tempted to blame current situations on the past. It seems a popular thing to do. I realize that what happens in our early years can be instrumental in forming the people we eventually become, but that doesn't give us excuses. You have power that is greater than my history, and You can help me to move beyond my circumstances to become the woman You've designed me to be.

Consider What You've Gained

But what things were gain to me, those I counted loss for Christ.
Yea doubtless, and I count all things but loss for the excellency of the
knowledge of Christ Jesus my Lord: for whom I have suffered the loss of all
things, and do count them but dung, that I may win Christ.

PHILIPPIANS 3:7–8

People have questioned the path I've taken, Lord. They wonder why I would spend so much effort on a college degree if I planned to work only a few years, then quit a good job to be home with my kids. I have no regrets. Those were good years, but Your plan is different for me now, and I'll do my best to raise my children in a way that will benefit Your kingdom.

Don't Be Quick to Judge

For we ourselves also were sometimes foolish, disobedient,
deceived, serving divers lusts and pleasures, living in
malice and envy, hateful, and hating one another.

TITUS 3:3

I can't count the number of times people have said, "Your daughter is just like you." I know it's true. She is a replica of everything good and bad that I was. So help me not to be too hard on her. You're not finished with me or her. Give both of us the grace to become like You, for we know we have been created in Your image.

I Was Blind but Now I See

He answered and said, Whether he be a sinner or no, I know not:
one thing I know, that, whereas I was blind, now I see.

JOHN 9:25

Your power is amazing; Your love is astonishing, dear God. People who were blind were given sight. Some who were lame were given strength to walk. Even some who were dead were given life. You altered the lives of these people so significantly that it was as though their pasts never existed. You did that for me too. Sin had blinded and crippled me, but You saved me from that wretched state and gave me new life. Thank You!

Remember Not the Sins of My Youth

Remember, O LORD, thy tender mercies and thy lovingkindnesses; for they have been ever of old. Remember not the sins of my youth, nor my transgressions: according to thy mercy remember thou me for thy goodness' sake, O LORD. Good and upright is the LORD: therefore will he teach sinners in the way. The meek will he guide in judgment: and the meek will he teach his way. All the paths of the LORD are mercy and truth unto such as keep his covenant and his testimonies.

PSALM 25:6–10

A Privileged Past

By faith Moses, when he was come to years, refused to be called the son of Pharaoh's daughter; choosing rather to suffer affliction with the people of God, than to enjoy the pleasures of sin for a season.

HEBREWS 11:24–25

Lord, Moses' story is so interesting. Apparently his mother used her time with him wisely, because he was willing to give up a life of great privilege to follow You. While I want to give my children the best I possibly can, I want them always to obey Your leading. I want them to love their family and their home, but I want them to love You more. Help me to set the right example for them.

From Horrible to Honorable

By faith the harlot Rahab perished not with them that
believed not, when she had received the spies with peace.

HEBREWS 11:31

If Rahab had known about "Faith's Hall of Fame," she
wouldn't have dared to hope she would be included. But
Lord, You didn't look at her hideous past. You saw her for
the person You would make her. You saved her from the
destruction of Jericho and from a life of prostitution. You
even allowed her to become a member of Christ's blood-
line. Thank You for also looking beyond my past to the person
You can make me.

Good but Not Enough

Brethren, I count not myself to have apprehended: but this
one thing I do, forgetting those things which are behind,
and reaching forth unto those things which are before.

PHILIPPIANS 3:13

"I fed my rabbit last night," my son pointed out, as if once-
in-a-while feedings were enough. I responded with, "I fed
you last night too." He seemed to get my point. It was a good
lesson to continue, so we talked about how reading Your
Word, praying, and serving You are good, but what we did
yesterday isn't enough. We need to walk with You daily. I pray
that we both benefit from this lesson.

Memorial Day

And this day shall be unto you for a memorial; and ye
shall keep it a feast to the LORD throughout your generations;
ye shall keep it a feast by an ordinance for ever.

EXODUS 12:14

On Memorial Day I love to sit at my kitchen table with my children. We make patriotic crafts, sing commemorative songs, and consider what we are remembering.

You established a memorial day for the Israelites thousands of years ago. They observed the day in remembrance of their rescue from Egypt. You rescued me too, Jesus. You pulled me from a life of sin and made me Your child. Make each day a memorial day of that wonderful event.

Don't You Remember?

*Do ye not yet understand, neither remember the five loaves
of the five thousand, and how many baskets ye took up?*

MATTHEW 16:9

You will always provide for the needs of my family, but sometimes I don't live like I believe it. How quickly I forget that You've always cared for me in the past. You've met my needs in ways I cannot fully comprehend. Yet I still worry about how the bills will be paid and how we'll manage all the "extras" that creep up. Forgive me, Lord. Help me to remember Your goodness and provision.

Passing It On

*One generation shall praise thy works to another,
and shall declare thy mighty acts.*

PSALM 145:4

Lord, if only everyone would consider all that You have done for us, we wouldn't be able to keep from praising You. I'm thankful You allowed me to have a Christian upbringing; I'm sure it contributed greatly to who I am today. Give me the wisdom to share this heritage with my children and to raise them in a godly way so they too will know You and pass on the torch of praise.

Used for Good

But as for you, ye thought evil against me; but God meant it unto good, to bring to pass, as it is this day, to save much people alive.

GENESIS 50:20

I've made some mistakes, God. I can't change them. Sometimes it seems they might control me, but I want to be controlled by You. Although I'm not happy about some of the choices I've made, I know You can turn them around and use them in a positive way. Lord, let this be the case.

My Future

The Power of Optimism

An elderly man lay peacefully on his deathbed surrounded by his loving family. Suddenly he became very excited. When asked what was happening, he exclaimed, "I see it! I can see heaven waiting for me!" When asked to describe it, he replied, "Oh, it's beautiful. More beautiful than any artist could possibly paint." Soon after, he joyfully entered heaven's glory.

Maybe this is how the apostle John felt as he wrote the book of Revelation. How could he, a mere mortal, possibly describe something so far beyond human comprehension? He did it, of course, with the help of the Holy Spirit, but with our finite minds we still comprehend only a glimmer of what awaits. Think of the most breathtaking place you've ever been. The beauty you envision is only a drop in the bucket compared to our future home. Not only that, but heaven is free of pain, suffering, worry, and all manner of earthly problems associated with sin and its effects. Yes, for the believer, the future is indeed bright.

The future includes an hour from now, tomorrow, next week, next year, and on through eternity. The future here on earth can be positive regardless of what is happening in your life. Maybe a new school year is about to begin. It seems most mothers approach this event with mixed feelings. They're a bit sad to be reminded of how quickly their little ones are growing up. They're anxious but hopeful that things will go well for their children during the coming year, and they're proud of how far their kids have come.

Our attitude toward the future tends to be based on a combination of past experiences, current circumstances, and the little we think we know of the future. Our attitude really should be based on knowing our future is in God's hands. We ought to be driven by a desire to obey God and let Him handle the details.

Think about the widow in 2 Kings 4. She had no income but considerable debt. The creditor had threatened to take her precious children as payment. So she sought Elisha. Giving no explanation, he said, "Borrow all your neighbors' pots and jars." Without questioning, she obeyed. God increased the bit of oil she had on hand so that she was able to sell it. She paid her debt and lived off the remainder of the profits. Her future had looked bleak, but faith and obedience gave her optimism. With God at our side, we too can be optimistic.

A Real Change

And that ye put on the new man, which after God
is created in righteousness and true holiness.

EPHESIANS 4:24

As I applied my makeup before church this morning, my young daughter asked about the purpose of each product. While I explained, I realized that in some ways I was giving a false impression of who I am. I wasn't really changing anything. I was just covering up the blemishes. I'm thankful, Lord, that when You do a work in me, it isn't simply cosmetic. You make me righteous and holy. The change is real.

For the Sake of the Elect

For then shall be great tribulation, such as was not since the
beginning of the world to this time, no, nor ever shall be.
And except those days should be shortened, there should no flesh
be saved: but for the elect's sake those days shall be shortened.

MATTHEW 24:21–22

Dear God, I love being a mother, but at times it nearly rips my heart out. Violence and promiscuity run rampant in society. I fear this world my children are growing up in, and I know it's only getting worse. As Christians we will find it more and more difficult to do what You've called us to do, but we know this time is temporary. Soon You will call us out of this mess into perfect eternity.

A Matter to Ponder

Keeping mercy for thousands, forgiving iniquity and transgression
and sin, and that will by no means clear the guilty; visiting the
iniquity of the fathers upon the children, and upon the children's
children, unto the third and to the fourth generation.

EXODUS 34:7

I heard a sermon about how our lives affect our family's future generations. The example of Jonathan Edwards was used. He was a great man of God, and many of his descendants were productive citizens. An outlaw whose name I can't even recall had many descendants who cost the nation a great deal of money. I know my children will choose their own paths, Lord. But the example I set will play a great role. Help me never to take my legacy lightly.

I Will Be with Thee

And he said, Certainly I will be with thee.
EXODUS 3:12

Each day holds something new, Father, and I don't always know what it will be. There are times when things have to be done, but one of the children wakes up with a fever or maybe I've misplaced my car keys. Sometimes I feel so overwhelmed that I don't want to know what lies ahead of me for the day or week. But You've promised that You will be with me—today and always.

Wings as Eagles

But they that wait upon the LORD shall renew their strength;
they shall mount up with wings as eagles; they shall run,
and not be weary; and they shall walk, and not faint.
ISAIAH 40:31

I've never seen a bald eagle in the wild, but I think someday I might because they've made an amazing comeback. There are times when I feel I need a recovery program too, dear Jesus. I am burdened down by the cares of this world, but I am trying to wait patiently. I know one day when the time is right, You'll give me wings like an eagle, and I'll soar to new heights.

Changing Address

Then we which are alive and remain shall be caught up
together with them in the clouds, to meet the Lord in
the air: and so shall we ever be with the Lord.

1 THESSALONIANS 4:17

My father often says we never actually die; we just change addresses. Those who've rejected You become eternal residents of hell. Those who've accepted You dwell eternally with You in heaven. I'm looking forward to that day. I've only changed my address once in my life. After hearing so many "moving day" horror stories, I'm thankful and glad that when I get to heaven, it will be for forever.

A Mystery

Behold, I shew you a mystery; We shall not
all sleep, but we shall all be changed.

1 CORINTHIANS 15:51

Oh, how I laughed the first time I saw this verse hanging above the changing table in the church nursery. It was just the humor this sleep-deprived mother needed. But God, there is so much promise in this simple passage. As a believer I have the hope that one day when life on earth ends, I will begin a new life in heaven and will be transformed into the image of Christ I'm meant to be.

Dreams and God

For in the multitude of dreams and many words
there are also divers vanities: but fear thou God.
ECCLESIASTES 5:7

As a child I can remember planning what I would be when I grew up. Oh, the list that I went through! Now it's fun to hear my children's thoughts and plans. I pray, dear God, that they would be sure to actively include You in their decisions. You have a perfect plan for each of them. Give them wisdom to understand that when You play the most significant role in the choices they make, that is when they'll be blessed.

Secret Things and Revealed Things

The secret things belong unto the LORD our God: but those
things which are revealed belong unto us and to our
children for ever, that we may do all the words of this law.
DEUTERONOMY 29:29

I know there are things You don't reveal to me about my future, dear God. I'm thankful for that. I'd likely be terrified if I could see everything. There are many things You have shown me though, so I will better serve and obey You and so my children will do likewise. Lord, let me please You all my days.

Waiting and Trusting

Lord, I'll not fret because of evildoers or be jealous of workers of iniquity. Soon enough they'll wither and fade. I'll trust in You and do good so that I may dwell in the land and be fed. I will delight myself in You, and You'll give me the desires of my heart. I'll commit my way to You and trust You. Your will is going to come to pass. You will lift up the righteous. I'll rest in You and wait patiently for You (Based on Psalm 37:1–7).

The End Is Near

And ye shall be hated of all men for my name's sake: but he that shall endure unto the end, the same shall be saved.
MARK 13:13

It sounds frightening, dear God. I know Satan is hard at work trying to discourage Christians and to keep us from serving You. Give us courage as we face the end-time challenges. Fill us with joy as we recognize we will soon see You face-to-face.

Seeing Christ

Yet a little while, and the world seeth me no more; but ye see me: because I live, ye shall live also.
JOHN 14:19

What a promise, Lord! It must have been hard for the disciples when they realized You were leaving them physically. I know how hard it was for me when my best friend moved thousands of miles away. I look forward to seeing her every few years, but it can't compare to the exhilaration of knowing that one day I will see You. Because You live, I live too.

The Prophecies

And Jacob called unto his sons, and said, Gather yourselves together, that I may tell you that which shall befall you in the last days.

GENESIS 49:1

Dear God, I find it interesting to read the blessings the biblical fathers placed before their sons. It's hard to understand how they could know what would happen, but as I read Jacob's final words to his sons, it's obvious that a lot of what he said was based on their past actions. Who we are today partly determines who we will become. Please give me wisdom to instill this truth in my children.

Revealed by the Spirit

But as it is written, Eye hath not seen, nor ear heard, neither have entered into the heart of man, the things which God hath prepared for them that love him. But God hath revealed them unto us by his Spirit: for the Spirit searcheth all things, yea, the deep things of God.

1 CORINTHIANS 2:9–10

"I'm not going to college," my five-year-old emphatically proclaimed. "Well, I am," retorted his younger sister. Not to be outdone, the three-year-old stated, "And I'm not getting married." They certainly have definite opinions, Lord. I just ask that as they accept You and draw closer to You they will pay attention to the guidance of Your Holy Spirit as they plan their futures. Please help them to do Your will.

Conclusion

The Power of Prayer

It is my hope that you have been blessed as you considered these passages of scripture and the prayers accompanying them. I pray that you have discovered or been reminded of the power that results from intimate conversation with our wonderful heavenly Father.

As mothers we view our time as very precious, and likely many of us schedule our day. Inevitably certain activities get bumped from our to-do lists. Often it's what we dislike the most that gets rejected. (Okay, I confess I detest folding laundry, and it's never hard to find something to take the place of that unpleasant task.) Sometimes the less urgent items get slashed. Too often this is where our time with God fits. We just don't see it as something that must be done.

If your house is full of children, things can get pretty hectic during their waking hours. Although you deeply love each arrow in your quiver (Psalm 127:4), you also value any quiet time you have before they rise in the morning and after they lie down at night.

How do you fill those rare quiet moments? Do you brew a cup of coffee and grab the morning paper? I know how lovely that can be, but consider limiting your newspaper reading to fill some of that time reading an uplifting psalm and talking to the One who can actually do something about depressing news stories. I understand that morning might not be your best time of day for serious devotions or in-depth Bible study, but a bit of time with the Lord will help get your day started right.

Throughout the day you are busy caring for your children and household duties. My guess is you've seen the many suggestions for how to pray through different chores or how to place nuggets of scripture in conspicuous places so that each time you see them, they will become more ingrained in your memory and your heart. When I was a young child in a Christian school, my mom would make up a tune to help me memorize verses. I've found those are the verses that stick with me now, and I've begun the same practice with my own children. We sing the verses together, and we're all hiding them in our hearts.

These ideas are all valid, but consider your own personality and circumstances when putting them into practice.

The same goes for prayer. As you teach your child to pray, you have an opportunity to talk to God as well. Have you ever listened to your child's prayer and noticed how similar it sounds to your own? Mealtime is a prime example. Does "Dear God, thank You for this food. Please bless it to our bodies" sound familiar? If such a prayer is part of your routine, then it's not really prayer. It could even be considered vain repetition, and as such it doesn't bring glory to God.

My three-year-old is learning to pray, and he generally uses the words, "Thank You, Jesus, for the food." This is true regardless of whether we're eating, preparing for bed, or doing something else. One night as he was saying this prayer before bed, I mentioned that it's good to thank Jesus for our food, but we really should thank Him for something besides food too. My son promptly bowed his head and said, "Thank You, Jesus, for something besides food."

I can't help chuckling each time I think about that, but at least he listened. When my five-year-old first began to pray, he consistently prayed about food as well. Now his prayers, though simple, are so heartfelt and beautiful they bring tears to my eyes. God doesn't mind that my child doesn't always use proper grammar or flowery words. He hears the thoughtful prayers from the heart.

Never underestimate the power of teaching your child to pray. You will grow in your own relationship with God. Your child also will begin to grow spiritually. As he does, he will begin to intercede to God on your behalf, and there is strength in intercessory prayer.

Perhaps you aren't at home during the day. You have many responsibilities that require your attention, and it's hard to find a spare moment for prayer and Bible reading. You admit that you need it, but you don't quite know how to fit it in. I used to like to pray out loud on my way to work. Praying out loud helped me concentrate on what I was saying, and it also kept me awake during those early morning drives. Those were probably some of the most meaningful prayers I ever uttered. I realize this isn't a good idea in every situation. If you are driving in a high-traffic area, your attention really can't be divided, but perhaps this suggestion will stir up other ideas that will work for you.

Unless all of your children are at school and you are home alone, devotions at midday might prove challenging. You might not be able to focus on a lengthy prayer period when the house is full of children, but why not take a few minutes before or after lunch? Choose a scripture promise and read it with your family. Then pray together, claiming God's promise for your lives. As your children grow older, take turns with them in leading these family prayers. You might be amazed at the spiritual depth your child exhibits, and it will be a time of growth for all of you.

The close of the day is another great time to commune with God. Even if the day has been particularly challenging, handing it over to God will give you a fresh perspective on it. Again, claiming His promises and thanking Him for His blessings is one of the best ways to get a restful sleep.

God is powerful. His answers to prayer offer abundant power, but we must pray. I pray the scripture passages in this book have offered you hope and encouraged you to look them up in context and to compose personal prayers. We are the children of the omnipotent heavenly Father. His power is limited only by our lack of faith in Him.

James 4:2 says, "Ye have not, because ye ask not." But that's only one verse of a larger passage. Look at the surrounding scripture. James points out that we seek many things in life and attempt to fulfill our desires in all the wrong ways. We need to become more involved with Jesus. When our hearts are right, we'll have proper desires and won't be ashamed to ask God to meet our needs.

Now look at James 4:6: "But he giveth more grace. Wherefore he saith, God resisteth the proud, but giveth grace unto the humble." Make sure you aren't too proud or busy to bow before God. It will take a bit of extra effort as a busy mom to take precious moments away from an already overflowing day, but it will be worth it for a life and a home filled with the power of God.

It cannot be emphasized enough that the moments invested with God are the most important moments you'll spend. We look at the awful things going on around us, and we cry, "Why doesn't someone do something about it?" The truth is that as more of us let God work within us as individuals, the more positive changes we will see in our communities and nation. Let Him start with you. Choose a time, place, and method for prayer and Bible reading. Stick with it, and continue to experience God's power in your life.

> *For our gospel came not unto you in word only, but also in power, and in the Holy Ghost, and in much assurance.*
> 1 THESSALONIANS 1:5

Scripture Index

PRAYER IS POWERFUL!

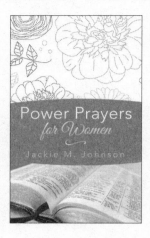

Power Prayers for Women

This practical and powerful guide helps readers pray
by offering solid biblical reasons to talk to God and
specific prayer starters for 21 key areas of life. Topics like
"My Emotions," "My Home," "My Finances," "My Fears,"
"My History," and "My Future" are addressed through
scripture and the life experiences of real women.

Paperback / 978-1-61626-948-7 / $4.99